ALL DONE FROM MEMORY

ALL DONE
FROM MEMORY

OSBERT LANCASTER

Illustrated by the Author

John Murray

First published in an autographed
edition limited to 45 copies in 1953.
This edition 1963

Printed in Great Britain
for John Murray, Albemarle Street, London
by Butler & Tanner Ltd., Frome and London

Je crois que le plus grand attrait des choses est dans le souvenir qu'elles réveillent dans le cœur ou dans l'esprit, mais surtout dans le cœur... Le regret du temps écoulé, le charme des jeunes années, la fraîcheur des premières impressions agissent plus sur moi que le spectacle même.

DELACROIX'S JOURNAL

My acknowledgements are due to the *Cornhill Magazine* in which the last two sections of this book were first published in their original versions.

Contents

DURING the ten or more years which have elapsed since this book was written, while I have indisputably grown both older and sadder, it would be unreasonable to assume that I have become any the wiser. So it seemed irrational to alter or amend; that those conclusions which today strike me as being rather too easily arrived at, or tinged with the dogmatism of early middle-age, would be better left unmodified; and that few portraits are likely to be rendered the more convincing by retouching.

O. L.

1963

OVERTURE

"Just a song at twilight"

I CANNOT honestly say that my attitude to flying-bombs was ever one of gay insouciance. Nevertheless as they grew more frequent I developed a paper-thin tolerance which I had never achieved during the earlier, more orthodox, bombardment. For one thing there was not, after the first few days, any anti-aircraft fire, which brought two advantages; first an unaccustomed quiet, and second, and more important, a welcome freedom of movement. During the 'blitz' so long as I remained indoors I was ceaselessly assailed by what psychiatrists so unfeelingly describe as 'irrational fears', but on escape into the wide open spaces these were promptly transformed by the patter of shrapnel into anxieties to which my reason accorded every justification. But during the short summer nights of 1944 it was possible to cut short the long hours of bedroom terrors by escaping into streets unmenaced by our own defences. And so it came about that on such evenings as I was not on duty I developed the habit of taking long walks through the misty Kensington evening and exploring districts which had for so long aroused my curiosity as to have acquired an almost fabulous quality but which in ordinary times I had never had the opportunity, or had lacked the energy, to penetrate.

The Holland Road which leads northward from my house is not in itself a romantic thoroughfare but the back-drop framed by the wings of its long stucco perspectives had always had for me a certain sinister fascination. A circular building in the style that the mid-Victorians were pleased to call Palladian marks the entrance to a narrow street of cheap shops running into the main road at an acute angle, crowded in peace-time with stalls and costers' barrows, which had always from earliest childhood strangely affected my imagination. In part this was due to an occasion when my father had, as a great treat, taken me to the White City Exhibition and we had halted here on our return to enjoy the spectacle of the seething Saturday night crowds, the women all in tight sealskin jackets and vast plumed hats, the men in pearl-buttoned waistcoats and flared trousers, jostling round the street-market in the theatrical light of the gas-jets; in part to the mystery and surprise which always colours any sudden revelation of a crowded slum-life existing behind a pompous and familiar façade and which is as powerfully induced by suddenly coming on one of the tenement streets which emerge between the neo-Renaissance palazzi of Fifth Avenue as by the half-glimpse of the Venetian ghetto seen beneath the arch of the Merceria. Here, moreover, the romance had been much heightened by the fear and distaste for the neighbourhood beyond, to which the more nervous of my elders were accustomed from time to time to give whispered expression. For in my youth Notting Dale was held, not, I fancy, altogether unreasonably, as one of the most dangerous districts of London and it was confidently stated that it was impossible for a well-dressed man to walk the length of the Portobello Road and emerge intact.

So powerfully had the prevailing attitude reacted on my sub-conscious that, although I had never in fact had occasion to do so, I had never gone out of my way to investigate this Alsatia of North Kensington. Now, when it seemed probable that the more enterprising thugs would be exercising their calling, thanks to the favourable conditions provided by the blackout, in the profitable districts of W.1, and the more nervous would be deep in the Tube shelters, was surely the ideal time for this long postponed exploration.

The deeper I penetrated into the stucco wilderness, deserted save for an occasional pathetic figure weighed down by bedding hurrying through the drizzle to the Shepherd's Bush Tube Station, the more insistent did the past become. A certain plenitude of frosted glass and bold Victorian display-types, still characteristic of Dublin and the lower East Side of New York, but elsewhere in London long since submerged beneath a flood of chromium plate and modernistic sans-serif, was doubtless chiefly responsible, but in addition long buried memories of streets half-seen in the distance from my pram, as nurse cautiously skirted the fringe of this City

2

of the Plain on our way to Wormwood Scrubs in the hope of seeing Mr. Graham White go up in his new flying machine, played their part. As I drifted on in a vaguely north-eastern direction, ears cocked for overhead chugging, the sense of familiarity deepened and finally achieved its maximum intensity at the end of a curving street of dilapidated semi-detacheds, all peeling paint and crumbling volutes.

As I paused to take in this panorama of decay my attention was irresistibly, but apparently illogically, drawn to a house immediately opposite across the street. Separated from the pavement by a few square feet of trampled grass and sooty laurels, the brickwork of the low wall still bearing scars that marked the recent out-wrenching of railings for the armaments drive, it in no way differed from any of its neighbours; the pillared portico and debased but still classical mouldings marked it as having been originally intended for some solid family of the Victorian *bourgeoisie*; the marked disparity of the window-curtains on the various floors, all subtly different in their general cheapness and vulgarity, indicated that it now sheltered three or perhaps foru separate establishments. My glance travelling disdainfully across this depressing façade, marking the broken balustrade above the cornice, the hacked and blackened lime-trees, the half erased 79 on the dirty umber of the door-pillars that had once been cream, came finally and shockingly to rest on the street name attached to the garden wall—Elgin Crescent. This, I suddenly realised, was my birthplace.

In my subconscious eagerness to prolong my evening stroll, I must have walked right through the haunted district I had set out to explore and emerged into the once familiar playground of my childhood on the slopes of Notting Hill. The fact that I had done so all unawares, that I had passed the formerly so firmly established boundary line without for a moment realising it, spoke far more clearly of what had happened here in the last thirty years than could many volumes of social history. As I walked on up the hill, regardless for once of a flying-bomb now following the course of Ladbroke Grove seemingly only just above the chimney-pots,

3

I noticed with a certain proprietary satisfaction that the progress of decay had not been halted at Elgin Crescent; that the squares and terraces that had once formed the very Acropolis of Edwardian propriety grouped round the church had suffered a hardly less severe decline. Some of the most obvious signs of degradation were certainly the result of five years of war and common to all parts of London, but here this enforced neglect was clearly but a temporary acceleration of a continuous process. The vast stucco palaces of Kensington Park Road and the adjoining streets had long ago been converted into self-contained flats where an ever-increasing stream of refugees from every part of the once civilised world had found improvised homes, like the dark-age troglodytes who sheltered in the galleries and boxes of the Colosseum. Long, long before the outbreak of war these classical façades had already ceased to bear any relevance to the life that was lived behind them; the eminent K.C.s and the Masters of City Companies had already given place to Viennese professors and Indian students and bed-sitter business girls years before the first siren sounded. And yet I who was only on the threshold of middle-age could clearly remember the days when they flourished in all their intended glory. At that house on the corner I used to go to dancing classes; outside that imposing front-door I had watched the carriages setting down for a reception; and in that now denuded garden I had once played hide and seek.

Many times since that wet wartime evening I have pondered on the implications of the dismal transformation then so suddenly brought home to me. This was not, it seemed to me, just a case of a once fashionable district declining slowly into slumdom but rather the outward and visible sign of the disappearance of a whole culture; a disappearance, moreover, which no one seems to have noticed and for which no tears had been shed. For it is a curious fact the term 'upper-middle-class' used as a social classification should only have achieved its maximum currency at a time when that class, or rather the cultural pattern which it established, had completely vanished; that while all the other labels which attached to the social stratifications of late Victorian life retain in varying

5

degrees a certain relevance, this which is shiny from over-use by leader-writers and social analysts marks a completely empty drawer. The aristocracy and landed gentry, although Nationally Entrusted and sadly Thirkellised, are still, thank goodness, for all their constant complainings of extinction, visibly and abundantly there; the lower-middle-class is not only still with us but so enormously increased in numbers and influence as to impose its own colour and standards on our whole civilisation; the working-class although, anyhow in London, being rapidly reduced by the ever-increasing rate of its absorption into the lower-middle-class and steadily losing much of its peculiar character remains numerous and powerful. But the old upper-middles, in so far as they possessed a definite culture and set of values of their own, are as extinct as the speakers of Cornish.

It is customary to explain this disappearance either in terms of the Marxian dialectic or by reference to the immense burden of taxation which weighed on them more heavily than on any other section of the community. It can also be correctly maintained that the continuous process of social assimilation, based on a deep-rooted national instinct that bids us reject on the one hand the transatlantic vision of the equality of man and on the other all the continental foolishness of *Ebenburtigkeit* and sixty-four quarterings, has been immeasurably accelerated in the last fifty years. Whereas a couple of generations separated the mediaeval burgher from the Tudor squire and another couple intervened between the Tudor squire and the Stuart nobleman, in recent years the social barriers between class and class, which though always clearly marked were never happily insuperable, have often all been leapt in a single lifetime. But, although there has always been a two-way traffic, the probability is that only a very small proportion of the two and a half million direct descendants of John of Gaunt would not now be black balled for a suburban tennis club, and economic arguments remain as partial an explanation as dialectical materialism.

Far and away the most important single factor leading to the complete collapse of the upper-middle-class way of life was the invention of the internal combustion engine; for the coming of the motor-car made possible the 'week-end', and the week-end spelt doom. However formal may have been the religion of this section of the community, the whole pattern of their life, anyhow in London, yet centred round the church, and once the cohesive force exercised by 'Morning Prayer' became weakened by the disruptive influence of the golf-links and the week-end cottage the whole social organism collapsed into its individual units. Curiously enough one of the few who seems at the time to have been aware, doubtless purely intuitively, of what was afoot was His late Majesty King George V (always temperamentally far closer to the upper-middle-class than the aristocracy), for if we are to believe the memoirs of his eldest son, one of the chief of his many objections to the younger generation was based on their fondness for leaving London at week-ends.

The vacuum involuntarily created by Lord Nuffield and his peers was filled in two ways, of which only one was connected with the process of dissolution. The lure of the country, besides ruining the home-counties, created a new class whose way of life, although originally based in intent on the emulation of that of the landed gentry, was in fact far closer to that of the middle-class immediately below them. By the 'thirties the differences dividing the £10,000 a year stockbroker from his £800 a year clerk were all quantitative not qualitative. One lived in a gabled mansion standing in its own grounds at Sunningdale, the other in a semi-detached villa at Mitcham, but both residences were bogus Elizabethan and both householders caught the 8.28 every morning. The stockbroker had a six-cylindered Rolls and a Lagonda, the clerk a second-hand Morris, but both were as likely as not to spend Sunday on the golf-links. They saw the same films, listened to the same radio-programmes, read the same newspapers, and neither of them went near a church except to get married. The way of life of both was equally far removed from that of the stock-broker's father living in Egerton Gardens or Orme Square.

The second, and perhaps more extraordinary, of the twentieth-century inventions which remoulded English social life was that of the intelligentsia. Hitherto, this amenity so long established on the continent had here been lacking. In Victorian times writers and artists, save for one or two of the most exalted, living remote and inaccessible on private Sinais in the Isle of Wight or Cheyne Row, had conformed to the pattern of the upper-middle-class to which most of them belonged. Matthew Arnold, Browning, Millais were all indistinguishable in appearance and behaviour from the great army of Victorian clubmen, and took very good care that this should be so. The *haute Bohème* did not exist and the Athenaeum rather than the Closerie des Lilas shaped the social life of the literary world. Only at the very end of the century amidst the gilded mirrors of the Café Royal did there emerge a society which bore some faint resemblance to those which had long been flourishing in the life of Paris, Vienna and Berlin; and even this, by the equal importance that sporting peers and racing journalists—the 'Pink'un' world in fact—enjoyed along with the artists and writers to whom they were linked by such liaison figures as Phil May and a common devotion to the Music Hall, bore a peculiar British stamp.

By the time the 'twenties were half-way through the whole picture had completely changed. The immense increase in size and circulation of newspapers and magazines, the rapid development of the cinema industry, the coming of the B.B.C., the colossal expansion of advertising, and later, the establishment of such organisations as the British Council, had transformed the pocket *Vie de Bohème*, which flourished in the late 'nineties into a vast army of salaried culture-hounds, an army which recruited its main strength from the younger generation of the upper-middle-class.

Unlike all the earlier class divisions the intelligentsia forms a vertical rather than a horizontal section of the community. Connecting at the top with the world of artistic dukes and musical minor royalty it trails away at the bottom into the lower depths of communist advertising men and *avant-garde* film directors. But however different the social and financial standing of the various grades within the group may be, the pattern of their existence remains strangely consistent and utterly at variance with that of the old middle-class from which so many of the members sprang. Where the parents, even those in some way connected with the arts, lived in substantial houses in which they ate regular meals the children live in flats and eat at snack-bars and restaurants; while the fathers not infrequently tended to look rather over-dressed in the country the sons invariably appear underdressed in the town. A society which was predominantly Anglican with a handful of high-minded agnostics has been transformed into one which is predominantly agnostic with a handful of not so high-minded Roman Catholics. For the transformation is widespread and complete. So successfully was the New Bohemia glamourised by female novelists during the 'twenties and 'thirties that its way of life has gladly been adopted by thousands of the old upper-middles whose connection with the arts is non-existent. Thus even so late as twenty years ago one was fairly safe in assuming that any bearded figure in corduroys reading the *New Statesman* was at very least a photographer or a museum official, whereas now he is just as likely to be a chartered accountant or a dry-salter. In a world where only Guards officers and bookmakers still maintain a sartorial standard, the social ideals of Murger are everywhere triumphant and even ordained ministers of the Established Church do not hesitate to advertise their broad-mindedness with soft collars and grey flannel 'bags'.

Although the effects of the change did not become generally apparent until after the first German War it was, in fact, well under way by 1914; but due largely to the patriarchal organisation of my family I was the fortunate victim of a time-lag and in the halls of my youth there still flourished a way of life which in more sophisticated circles was already in visible dissolution. From the death of the old Queen until the outbreak of war this small society upheld the standards of Victorianism with the same unruffled tenacity with which the Sephardic community at Salonika persisted in speaking fifteenth-century Spanish; fully aware of Bernard Shaw, Diaghilev and Alexander's Ragtime Band their outlook remained as resolutely unmodified by these phenomena as that of the Adobe Indians by the airplane and the radio.

The present volume is not, therefore, primarily autobiographical in intent but rather, by using thematic material drawn from a few commonplace incidents of childhood, an attempt to raise not a monument but a small memorial plaque to a vanished world. Many of the principal characters may well appear to readers below the age of forty ridiculous, maladjusted and anachronistic, wilfully blind to the great changes going on about them and rashly presumptuous in their firm convictions. Such a view is easily justifiable and, indeed, is one which I myself frequently expressed in my heedless youth. But, sheltering from the chugging menace overhead in the shabby ruins of their citadel scrawled with slogans demanding a Second Front and scarred by blast yet still retaining in the evening light an almost Venetian grandeur of decay, self-confidence waned. Whether their disappearance is an irreparable loss or a welcome deliverance I am too close to them to say: I can only record that I have become increasingly conscious of the debt, which, for good or ill, I owe them.

1. *"Take me back to dear old Shepherd's Bush"*

I WAS BORN in the eighth year of the reign of King Edward the Seventh in the parish of St. John's, Notting Hill. At that time Elgin Crescent, the actual scene of this event, was situated on the Marches of respectability. Up the hill to the south, tree-shaded and freshly stuccoed, stretched the squares and terraces of the last great stronghold of Victorian propriety: below to the north lay the courts and alleys of Notting Dale, through which, so my nurse terrifyingly assured me, policemen could only proceed in pairs.

The Crescent, like all border districts, was distinguished by a certain colourful mixture in its inhabitants, lacking in the more securely sheltered central area, grouped in this case round the church. While residence there was socially approved and no traces of 'slumminess' were as yet apparent, there did cling to it a slight whiff of Bohemianism from which Kensington Park Road, for instance, was quite free. Of the residents several were connected with the Stage, and some were foreign, but neither group carried these eccentricities to excessive lengths. Among the former were numbered a Mr. Maskelyne (or was it a Mr. Devant?) who lived on the corner, and, right next door to us, the talented authoress of *Where the Rainbow Ends*, whose daughter, a dashing hobble-skirted croquet-player, remains a vivid memory. The foreigners included some Japanese diplomats and a German family connected with the Embassy, whose son, a fair, chinless youth, was always at great pains to model his appearance on that of the Crown Prince Wilhelm, much to the delight of my father whom a long residence in Berlin had rendered expert in detecting the subtlest nuances of this elaborate masquerade. Fortunately my parents' arrival at Number 79 had done much to erase the principal blot on the fair name of the street, as our house had previously been the home of no less equivocal a figure than Madame Blavatsky.

Number 79 was a semi-detached stucco residence on three floors and a basement with a pillared porch, not differing stylistically in any way from the prevailing classicism of the neighbourhood. At the back was a small private garden opening into the large garden common to all the occupants of the south side of Elgin Crescent and the north side of Lansdowne Road. Such communal gardens, which are among the most attractive features of Victorian town-planning, are not uncommon in the residential districts of West London, but are carried to the highest point of their development in the Ladbroke estate. This area, which was laid out after the closure of the race-course that for a brief period encircled the summit of the hill, represents the last rational, unselfconscious piece of urban development in London. It was unfortunately dogged by misfortune, and the socially ambitious intention of Allom, the architect, and the promoters was largely defeated by the proximity of an existing pottery slum in Notting Dale, which received, just at the time the scheme was being launched, an enormous and deplorable influx of Irish labourers working on the Great Western Railway.

How different it all was in the years before 1914! Then the stucco, creamy and bright, gleamed softly beneath what seems in reminiscence to have been a perpetually cloudless sky. Geraniums in urns flanked each brass-enriched front door, while over the area railings moustachioed policemen made love to buxom cooks. And in every street there hung, all summer long, the heavy scent of limes.

The angel who drove the original inhabitants out of this gilt-edged Eden, not with a flaming sword but by a simple vanishing trick, was the domestic servant. The houses, even the small ones like ours, were planned on generous lines and labour-saving was still not only an unrealised but un-thought-of ideal. Fortunately my parents, whose joint income at the time of my birth amounted to all of £600 a year, were able to maintain a cook, a housemaid, a nurse and a boot-boy; my mother, moreover, had been through the hard school of a Victorian grandmother's household, and herself undertook such specialised, and now obsolete, labours as cleaning the chandeliers, washing the rubber-plant and superintending the linen.

The ideal of the servantless civilisation, already fully realised in the United States, is doubtless a noble one, and those who so bravely, and possibly sincerely, maintain that they feel degraded by being waited on by their fellow human beings compel our admiration, although personally they invariably provoke me to confess that I can tolerate without discomfort being waited on hand and foot. But it is an ideal attended by one grave disadvantage—whom is there left for the children to talk to? A mother's love is all very well, but it is only a poor substitute for good relations with the cook.

In my own case, the centre of the below-stairs world was Kate the housemaid. This remarkable woman, gaunt, near-sighted and invariably prepared for the worst, not only endeared herself to me by acts of kindness to which I could always be certain no strings were attached, but also provided my only contact with the real world which lay beyond the confines of my isolated nursery. Quick-witted and an omnivorous reader of the popular press, it was her habit to converse largely in political slogans and popular catch-phrases. Thus when I was detected sliding unobtrusively into the larder she would call out "Hands off the people's food", and if when driven out she suspected that I still retained some loot she would advance with simulated menace, jabbing the upturned palm of her left hand with the index finger of her right, in a gesture which a dozen cartoons of the then Chancellor of the Exchequer,

Mr. Lloyd George, had rendered universally familiar, exclaiming "Put it there!" And always when I asked what was for dinner she would remind me of Mr. Asquith and bid me "Wait and see". But by no means all of her sources of verbal inspiration were political; better even than the Harmsworth Press she loved the music-hall, and her evenings off were regularly spent at one or other of the many suburban houses then still happily flourishing on the sites of future Odeons. Her favourite performers were Wilkie Bard, George Mozart and Alfred Lester, and while engaged on her endless scrubbing and dusting she could usually be heard informing the household that she had got a motto, or wanted to sing in opera, or desired to be taken back to dear old Shepherd's Bush.

The popular music of the Edwardian era played an important rôle in the national life: these music-hall songs and ballads have today been so weakened and degraded by intensive plugging and self-conscious revival over the air that they are now as far removed from their former spontaneous popularity as are the careful prancings of latter-day Morris dancers from the village revels of the Elizabethans. In the strictly stratified social world of my childhood they seemed to me in my bourgeois pram to be the one thing enjoyed in common by the world represented by the whistling errand-boy and the ladies I occasionally observed, humming gaily, if a little off-key, as they emerged from the glittering paradise of *The Devonshire Arms* (in passing which my nurse always developed an additional turn of speed and on which she would never comment), and the world of which the pillars were Kate and my father. I specify my father rather than my parents as his taste was almost identical with Kate's (he perhaps rated Harry Lauder a little higher than she did), whereas my mother's was more accurately represented by *Traumerei* and *Songe d'automne*, beautiful works, doubtless, but hardly with so universal an appeal.

A few additional figures there were who stood in a rather closer relation to the small world of Number 79 than the anonymous ranks of passers-by I observed from my pram: they, while obviously debarred from the full club privileges of Kate, the cook, my parents and the boot-boy, yet enjoyed, as it were, the facilities of country membership. The Italian organ-grinder, a martyr to gastric troubles, who regularly appeared every Thursday afternoon; the crossing-sweeper in Ladbroke Grove whose function the internal combustion engine was even then rapidly rendering as decorative as that of the King's Champion; the muffin man, the lamplighter and the old gentleman who came out on winter

evenings to play the harp by the foggy radiance of the street lamp —Dickensian figures who have obviously no rôle to play in the Welfare State and have left no successors. Doubtless their disappearance should be welcomed, and yet they did not appear to be either downtrodden or exploited: indeed, the impression they gave was chiefly of a proper consciousness of the important rôle in the social fabric played by muffin men, lamplighters and organ-grinders. Certainly their spirits seemed higher and their manners were undoubtedly better than those of the majority of the present-day beneficiaries of enlightened social legislation. Even the crossing-sweeper, despite his ostentatious rags and traditional whine, displayed a certain individuality and professional pride which one seldom observes in the hygenically-uniformed Municipal Refuse Disposal Officer.

Apart from such figures, my relations and, later, fellow-pupils at my kindergarten, the most vivid and indirectly influential personality of my early childhood was our next-door neighbour to the west, old Mrs. Ullathorne. This imposing and always slightly mysterious *grande dame*, with whom I was bidden to tea at regular intervals, represented an era which, even at that date, seemed almost incredibly remote. She had enjoyed, so it was said, a considerable success at the court of Napoleon the Third, and there were prominently displayed amongst the palms and bibelots of her crowded drawing-room innumerable *carte-de-visite* size photographs of dashing cuirassiers in peg-top trousers sporting waxed moustaches and elegant lip-beards, and of crinolined beauties who had somewhat surprisingly elected to put on full ball-dress and all their diamonds for a good long read, of what appeared from the binding to be books of devotion, seated on rustic benches in a vaguely Alpine landscape. Certainly Mrs. Ullathorne herself gave a very definite impression of belonging to another, and far more sophisticated, world than that of Edwardian Notting Hill. Alone among all our female acquaintances she was heavily and unashamedly made-up (even the dashing daughter of our playwright neighbour, who was thought to be a suffragette and known to smoke, never, I fancy, went further than a discreet use of *papiers poudrés*). But the style in which her *maquillage* was conceived proclaimed her way behind, rather than daringly ahead, of the times. The whole surface of her face was delicately pale and matt, and only by imperceptible degrees did the pearly white take on a faint rosy flush above the cheekbones; the eyebrows, which although carefully shaped were not plucked thin, were a deep uncompromising auburn, contrasting very strikingly with the faded parma violet of the lids. Her toupet, a rich mahogany in colour, was dressed in tight curls and fringes in the manner of the reigning queen. The whole effect was one of extreme fragility which, one felt, the slightest contact or even a sneeze would irretrievably wreck, and was as far removed from that achieved by modern methods as is a Nattier from a Modigliani.

Whether due to Mrs. Ullathorne's long residence in foreign parts or to her extreme age, she displayed another peculiarity which set her still further apart from the rest of my world—she invariably insisted that in place of the customary handshake I should bow smartly from the waist and kiss her hand. This was for me always rather an alarming ordeal, and I can still see that long white hand delicately extended, criss-crossed with the purple hawsers of her veins standing out in as high relief as the yellowish diamonds in her many rings, and experience once more the ghastly apprehension that one day, overcome by unbearable curiosity, I should take a sharp nip at the most prominent of those vital pipelines.

The influence which the old lady exercised on my early development was not, however, direct, but the result of a gift. One day she presented me with a large quarto volume bound in dark green leather into which, with incredible neatness, she had in childhood pasted scraps.

Although I can still vividly remember the enchantment which was renewed every time I opened that magic volume, it is only quite fortuitously that its peculiar flavour, recognisable if faint, now and then returns to me. No effort of conscious memory will work the miracle, but just occasionally the sight of swans upon a castle lake, or some peculiar combination of Prussian blue and carmine, or the feel beneath the fingers of the embossed paper lace on an old-fashioned Christmas card, will play the part of Proust's Madeleine and fire the train. Many must have received such volumes in childhood, but not many I fancy so perfect an example of the genre as this; for the artists of no age have ever surpassed those of the romantic period in the production of keepsakes and *culs-de-lampes*, and this volume had been compiled at exactly the right moment. The shakoed, hand-coloured infantryman, who so gallantly assaulted that vaguely Oriental stronghold, were the soldiers of Louis Philippe subduing the fierce Goums of Ab-del-Kedir; this mysterious steel-engraved lake shadowed by twilit mountains was Lamartine; and the rather over-plumed knights, their armour gleaming with applied tinsel, were undoubtedly setting out for the Eglinton Tournament.

The charm and excitement of those vividly coloured vignettes must have made a powerful appeal to the imagination of any child but in my case it was reinforced by the contrast they provided to the illustrations in my other books. My mother suffered from that perpetual illusion common to all parents that the books which had meant the most to her in her own childhood (or possibly those which, later in life, she had persuaded herself had then been her favourites) would awaken a similar delighted response in her off-spring. My nursery library was therefore well stocked with the illustrated fairy-tales of the late 'seventies and early 'eighties. It cannot be denied that the skill of the great nineteenth-century school of English wood-engraving was then at its height and that many of these volumes were, in their way, masterpieces. Nevertheless, not only did I dislike them all with the solitary exception of Tenniel's *Alice*, but certain of them awoke in me feelings of fear and revulsion.

I do not think, looking back, that my reaction was purely personal nor wholly abnormal. Children are all firmly in favour of representational art up to a certain point (my lack of enthusiasm for Walter Crane, for instance, was caused by his tendency to subordinate accurate representation to decorative embroidery and was of a wholly different kind to my dislike of Linley Sambourne), but that point is reached when realism is carried over into the third dimension. They will welcome, and indeed demand, the maximum amount of realistic detail provided it is flat, but once an artist starts to give his illustrations depth and to visualise his figures in the round, his pre-adolescent public will begin to lose interest. Thanks to the incredibly responsive instrument which such figures as the Dalziels had made of the wood-engraver, the book illustrators of the 'eighties were able to exploit the third dimension, which still possessed in this medium the charm of comparative novelty, to their hearts' content, and they certainly made the most of the opportunity. The buxom flanks of the Water Babies sprang from the flat page with a startling illusion of rotundity; the more unpleasant creations of Hans Andersen's imagination displayed a devastating solidity; indeed, certain artists went rather too far in their three-dimensional enthusiasm and overstepping the bounds of realism achieved an effect which can only be described, in the strictest sense of the word, as surrealist. In our own day this irrational element in the wood-engraved illustrations of the late nineteenth century, against which I as a child had unconsciously reacted (in exactly the same way, incidentally, as did my own children some twenty-five years later), has been recognised and skilfully utilised for his own terrifying purposes by Max Ernst in such works as 'Le Lion de Belfort' and 'La Femme a cent têtes'.

Thus the world of Mrs. Ullathorne's scrap-book, with its brilliant green lawns and flat improbable trees peopled by kindly gendarmes in enormous tricornes and little girls in pork-pie hats and striped stockings practising archery in château parks, took on in addition to its own proper attraction the welcome character of a safe retreat from that other, boring yet terrifying, world of all too completely realised fantasy.

The work from which, next to the scrap-book, I derived the greatest enjoyment was also uncontemporary, being two bound volumes of the *Picture Magazine*, to which my father had regularly subscribed during his school days at the very end of the Victorian age. This admirable periodical nicely combined instruction with amusement, and among the regular features were a series of simple pseudo-scientific experiments (a cock mesmerised into following a chalked line with its beak and a daring criminal escaping from Vincennes by means of a home-made parachute), accounts of travel and exploration (whiskered tourists being hauled up to the monasteries of the Meteora in nets), and, best of all, strip cartoons by Caran d'Ache. In addition were included from time to time four-page supplements of photographs of the most distinguished figures in one particular walk of contemporary life—soldiers, scientists, painters . . . Of these my favourite was that devoted to the rulers of sovereign states who, thank Heaven, were at that date far more numerous than they are today.

Those long rows of royal torsos adorned with every variety of epaulette, plastron, and aiguillette, the necks compressed into collars of unbelievable height and tightness, the manly, if padded chests, hung with row upon row of improbable crosses and stars and criss-crossed by watered silk ribbons and tangles of gold cords, surmounted by so many extraordinary countenances adorned with immense moustaches, upstanding in the style of Potsdam or down-sweeping in the style of Vienna, some fish-eyed, some monocled, some vacant, some indignant but all self-conscious, had for me a fascination which never failed. And nor, when I had learnt to read, did the captions prove a disappointment; such names as Mecklenberg-Schwerin, Bourbon-Parme, Saxe-Coburg-Gotha held for me a flavour of high romance to which the very difficulty of pronouncing added rather than detracted. How drab by contrast did the still small handful of republican presidents appear, and how deep was my contempt for those pince-nezed, bourgeois figures to whom a gaudy silken diagonal across their stiff-shirted bosoms could not lend an air of even spurious distinction!

Incredible as it may seem, many of these paladins who now appear far more remote from our modern experience than Attila or Ivan the Terrible were actually still more or less firmly on their thrones at the time when I first grew familiar with their appearance. The whiskered porcine features of Franz Josef were still regularly revealed to his loyal Viennese as he drove every morning through the Hofburg; hardly a day passed without his German colleague, dressed as an Admiral, a Hussar, a Uhlan, a Cuirassier, or a Highland sportsman, making an appearance in the illustrated papers; and somewhere hidden away in the heart of the plaster mazes of Dolmabâghcheh, that last bastard offspring of a frenzied rococo which had reared itself so surprisingly on the shores of the Bosphorus, apprehensive, invisible but undoubtedly there, was Abdul the Damned.

Of all this I was at that time naturally unaware. All these characters were no more and no less real to me than Jack the Giant-Killer and the Infant Samuel of whom my mother was accustomed to read aloud, or Hackenschmidt and the Terrible Turk, in whose exploits the boot-boy took so keen an interest. Only Kaiser Wilhelm was for me in any way, and that very remotely, connected with real life; for I had once been sent a box of toy soldiers by an old friend of my mother, who was one of that monarch's A.D.C.s, and whose photograph in the full-dress uniform of the Prussian Guard stood on the piano.

Less colourful but more familiar were the pages devoted to the more prominent contemporary divines. No flourishing moustachios nor jewelled orders here, but every variety of whisker from the restrained mutton-chop to the full Newgate fringe, and billowing acres of episcopal lawn. At the time these portraits were taken the social prestige of the Establishment, and even, on a different level, of Nonconformity, was at its height, and although it had become a little dimmed in the intervening years it was still comparatively great. How complete has been the subsequent eclipse, a brief study of the representative novels of high life during the last half century will amply demonstrate; although the regiments of handsome curates, worldly Archdeacons and courtly Bishops who thronged the pages of late Victorian fiction thinned out a lot in Edwardian times, a sharp-tongued Mayfair incumbent or two, ex-curates doubtless of Canon Chasuble, still make a regular appearance in the tales of Saki: but in all the works of Michael Arlen I cannot recall a single dog-collar and the solitary cleric to appear in the novels of Mr. Waugh is Fr. Rothschild, S.J.

In real life, anyhow in the society in which my parents moved, the clergy still played a prominent and honoured rôle. Their merits as preachers were eagerly discussed and the exact degree of their 'Highness' or 'Lowness' keenly debated. Many of the originals of those portraits were, therefore, quite familiar to me by name as being preachers under whom members of my family had at one time or another sat, while on the knees of one of them, Prebendary Webb-Peploe, a celebrated Evangelical preacher from whose well-attended Watch Night sermons the more impressionable members of the congregation were regularly carried out on stretchers, I myself had once had the honour of being perched.

It may seem strange that my infant literature should have been so exclusively out-of-date, but at that time the modern renaissance of the children's book was in its infancy, and the prevailing standard of contemporary productions was unbelievably low. Exceptions there were, however, and I can vividly remember the pleasure I derived from the Nursery History of England, illustrated by that happily still flourishing artist, George Morrow, and, a little later, from the works of Edmund Dulac.

To the enjoyment of the pictures, appreciation of the text was soon added, as thanks to the brilliant educational methods of my mother I learned to read at a very tender age. Her system, simple as it was effective, was based on a chocolate alphabet. This was spread out twice a week on the dining-room table and such letters as I recognised I was allowed to eat; later, when my knowledge of the alphabet was faultless, I was entitled to such letters as I could form into a new word. Although never strong in arithmetic I soon grasped the simple fact that the longer the word the more the chocolate, and by the time I could spell 'suffragette' without an error this branch of my education was deemed complete and a tendency to biliousness had become increasingly apparent.

Once my ability was firmly established I read everything on which I could lay my hands, from *The Times* leaders to the preface to the Book of Common Prayer. This impressive zeal was not, I fancy, the result of any exceptional thirst for knowledge, but rather of boredom, and was far commoner among children at that time than it is today. Such cinemas as then existed were regarded by my parents as undesirably sensational and notoriously unhygienic, and there was no compulsion on grown-ups to make any pretence of enjoying the company of the young who were, quite rightly, expected to amuse themselves. The only addition which modern science had made to the sources of infant pleasure available to my parents, or even my grandparents, was the gramophone. On this archaic machine I was permitted, as a great treat, to listen to the exaggeratedly Scots voice of Harry Lauder, just audible through a barrage of scratching and whining, singing 'Stop your tickling, Jock', or to the waltzes of Archibald Joyce rendered, rather surprisingly, by the Earl of Lonsdale's private band and recorded on discs half an inch thick by Messrs. William Whiteley.

My appearances in the drawing-room, where the gramophone was kept, were determined in accordance with fixed rules, as indeed were those of almost all the children of my generation—on weekdays half an hour before going to bed and half an hour in the morning to practise my scales, the latter period being prolonged to an hour on Tuesdays when Miss Pearce, poor long-suffering woman, came to wrestle with my highly personal rendering of 'The Merry Peasant'. Apart from these daily occasions, the only times when the room knew me were when there were visitors.

The pattern of social life in archaic Bayswater, and all points west, differed almost as much from that prevailing today as it did from that of mediaeval times. Fixed rules prevailed governing the exact hours and days on which visits took place, the number and size of the cards left and when and how they should be 'cornered', the clothes to be worn, and the length of time which one was expected to stay; even such trivial gestures as those with which the ladies, once perched on the Edwardian Hepplewhite chairs, were accustomed to throw back their veils and roll down their gloves at the wrists, were formal and standardised. There was no casual dropping-in for drinks, as drinking between meals was confined exclusively to the restorative masculine whisky-and-soda (or among the older generation "a little b. and s.")—almost exclusively, for curiously enough I do recollect among certain of my older female relatives the ritual partaking of a glass of port wine and a slice of plum cake at eleven o'clock in the morning, although this was generally regarded as an old-fashioned survival only to be justified on grounds of old age or a delicate constitution. There was no ringing up and asking people round for a little cocktail party as we had no telephone and cocktails were still unknown, save perhaps to certain rather 'fast' Americans—the sort of people who patronised those 'tango teas' of which the papers spoke.

Where no casual appearance could possibly take place, and all was fixed and pre-ordained, I knew exactly when the summons to present myself below would come. My mother, like all the ladies of her acquaintance, had her Thursdays, when the silver teapot and the best china would be shiningly conspicuous and her friends and relations would dutifully appear to be entertained with cucumber sandwiches, *petit-fours*, slices of chocolate cake and, in winter, toasted buns. Those who could not come, either because the number of their friends who had also chosen Thursday as their 'At Home' day precluded a personal appearance at each or for some other valid reason, sent round their cards.

My own entry was always carefully timed by Nurse to coincide with the moment when the teacups, with which I was hardly to be trusted, were already distributed and the sandwiches and cakes were waiting to be handed round. My performance on these occasions was invariably masterly. Clad in a *soigné* little blue silk number, with Brussels lace collar and cut steel buckles on my shoes, in which I had recently made my first public appearance as a page at a wedding in All Saints, Margaret Street, I passed round the solids in a manner which combined efficiency with diffidence in exactly the right proportions. Moreover, although conspicuously well-behaved, I could always be relied on to go into the *enfant terrible* act at exactly the right moment, and produce embarrassing questions or comments of a laughable kind that yet just stopped short of being offensively personal or too outspokenly apt. The freely expressed admiration which my performance always produced was almost as gratifying to me as it was to my mother, particularly in such cases where I considered it was likely to pay a handsome dividend next Christmas. Only among my Lancaster relations was the rapture apt to be a little modified; my Aunt Hetty, for instance, was more than once heard to remark that if Mamie were not careful dear little Osbert would soon be developing a deplorable tendency to "play to the gallery".

The only other times (apart from the many-coursed dinner parties of the period, a fixed number of which my parents were accustomed to give during the year, which naturally affected my

life not at all) on which visitors appeared was when country relatives were in London and were of sufficient age or importance to be asked to tea or luncheon for themselves alone. The most memorable of these was my Great Aunt Martha, not only for her own personality and appearance which were remarkable enough, but also for the manner of her arrival. Having been born early in the reign of George IV she was relatively fixed in her ways, and when she came to stay with her younger brother, my grandfather, the victoria and the greys were put at her disposal: their use in London had otherwise come to be increasingly abandoned in favour of the Renault, and they were only still maintained, I fancy, out of respect for Mundy, the elderly coachman, and a deep-rooted enthusiasm for harness horses which was general in my father's family.

I can still recall the stately dignified clop-clop, quite different in rhythm from that of the brisk single-horsed baker's van or the heavy proletarian tattoo of the pantechnicon, which announced that Aunt Martha was rounding the corner, and which I had been eagerly awaiting at the nursery window for half an hour or more. Quickly snatching up some lumps of sugar from Nurse, I was down the stairs and at the horses' heads almost before the footman was off the box. Looking back, I confess myself lost in admiration at my youthful temerity, as nowadays my reluctance to go fumbling round the muzzles of relatively unfamiliar quadrupeds would hardly be so easily overcome.

Great Aunt Martha, although even older than Mrs. Ullathorne, gave no such impression of fragility; on the contrary she appeared, and indeed she was, exceedingly robust and just about as fragile as well-seasoned teak. Her eyebrows which were thick as doormats were jet-black and her hair, which she wore severely parted in the middle and swept smoothly down over each cheek, was only streaked with grey. She never appeared abroad save in the prescribed Victorian uniform for old ladies—black bonnet enriched with violets, a black jet-trimmed shoulder cape and very tight black kid gloves—which was becoming increasingly rare even at that date and now only survives among pantomime dames. Her features were strong and masculine and bore a close resemblance to those of Sir Robert Walpole as revealed in Van Loos' portrait, and she retained a marked Norfolk accent. Tolerant and composed, she radiated an air of genial and robust common sense, which none of the rest of the family displayed, anyhow in so marked a degree; and alone of all the Lancasters she professed a keen interest in food and was reputed to be the finest hand with a dumpling between King's Lynn and Norwich. In addition she was never at any pains to conceal an earthy relish for scandal which, linked to a prodigious memory, made her a far more entertaining, and quite possibly a more accurate, authority on the genealogies of most Norfolk families than Burke.

Despite her outward Victorianism, Great Aunt Martha nevertheless always gave a strong but indefinable impression of belonging to a still earlier era. This must, I think, have arisen largely from her gestures, for gestures remain the surest and least easily eradicable of all period hall-marks. Tricks and turns of speech are good guides but are generally indetectable when combined with a strong regional accent; clothes and hair styles may be deliberately and consciously adopted for their period value; but gestures are easy neither unconsciously to lose nor deliberately to acquire. One has only to compare the most accurate reconstruction of a 'twenties scene in a modern revue with a thirty-year-old film to appreciate this truth; no matter how skilfully the accents and fashions of the epoch may have been recaptured on the stage the film will always reveal a dozen little gestures—a peculiar fluttering of the hand or some trick of standing—which at the time were so natural as to be completely unnoticeable, and of which even the most knowledgeable spectator with an adult memory of the period and the keenest eye for detail will have remained completely unaware and may even, on seeing them again after a lapse of thirty years, fail to realise are the very hallmarks of that genuineness of which he is nevertheless completely convinced.

The particular gesture of Aunt Martha's which I found so revealing and which, had I not seen her so frequently employ it, I should have come to consider a stereotyped illustrator's convention, no more having an origin in nature than the Fascist salute or the sudden heart-clutching of an Italian tenor, was that with which she invariably registered surprise. This was an emotion constantly evoked in her by the unexpected brilliance (as she thought it) of her great-nephews and nieces or the extraordinary things of which the newspapers were nowadays so full. Maintaining her usual upright but placid attitude when seated, she would suddenly elevate her eyebrows to a remarkable height and in perfect unison raise her hands, which had been lying quietly in her lap, smartly at right angles to her wrists with palms outwards, at the same time, but more slowly, lifting her forearms until the tips of her outspread fingers were level with her shoulders, in a manner that was perfectly familiar to me from the illustrations of Cruickshank.

Such visits as those of Aunt Martha were, however, few and far between, and the rhythm of our daily life, monotonous as it would seem to a modern child, was but seldom interrupted by these intrusions from the outside world. Thus the drawing-room saw me chiefly in its familiar everyday dress, very different from the unnatural spruceness and formality it assumed on social occasions, and so it remains in my memory. Summoned down for my daily visit I would take my accustomed place beside my mother for the evening reading. My enjoyment at this performance depended in a very large measure on the choice of the book, which was governed partly by the day and partly by my mother's mood.

On Sundays and holy days, or on occasions when some recent display of temper or disobedience on my part was thought to have merited implied reproof, the volume chosen was a ghastly selection of pious fables, illustrated in that wood-engraved style I so much abominated. What particularly infuriated me about the author, and still infuriates me, was not so much his unctuous style, nor even the pious nature of the themes, but his abominable deceit. The hero, some gallant knight, would don his armour, leap on his trusty steed and go galloping off in pursuit of dragons in the most approved style, and then, just as my interest was getting aroused, it was revealed that the armour, on the exact style and manufacture of which I had been excitedly speculating, was the armour of Righteousness, the steed one learnt answered to the name of Perseverance, and the dragons against which the hero was off to do battle were called Self-Love, Indolence and Bad Temper. Thus one cold puff of piety instantly and irrevocably shattered the warm colourful world of romance and fantasy which had been building up in my imagination and my rage, though concealed, was boundless. But it was years before the sight of that thick little royal blue volume, so guileless and optimistic is the infant mind, warned me to expect the worst.

But in the course of time my so evident lack of response led to the gradual abandonment of this depressing volume, and the occasions on which I was firmly removed from the study of some illustrated volume of my own choice to listen to the far from hair-raising adventures of some smug paladin of evangelical piety became fewer and fewer. And in the picture which I chiefly retain of these early evenings of my childhood it plays no part.

The firelight is gleaming and flashing from the polished brass of the heavily defended hearth; on one side sits my father, freshly returned from the city, reading one of the pastel-coloured evening papers of the time; on the other my mother, studying with well-founded distrust the double-page spread of the interior of the newly-launched 'Titanic' in the *Illustrated London News*. The pleasantly depressing strains of 'The Count of Luxembourg', rendered of course by the Earl of Lonsdale's private band, faintly echo amidst the shiny chintz and gold-mounted watercolours, speaking of a far distant world of dashing Hussars and tight-waisted beauties in long white gloves with aigrettes in their golden hair, for ever dancing up and down some baroque staircase of exceptional length. While in the middle, flat on his stomach, lies a small boy of engaging appearance poring over an enormous green volume, the faintly dusty smell of the fur hearthrug heavy in his nostrils, perfectly happy counting the medals stretched across the manly chest of the Hereditary Prince of Hohenzollern Sigmaringen.

2. *"Has anyone seen a German Band?"*

FOR SHEER pleasure few methods of progression, one comes gradually to realise, can compare with the perambulator. The motion is agreeable, the range of vision extensive and one has always before one's eyes the rewarding spectacle of a grown-up maintaining prolonged physical exertion. Moreover, the sensation of pasha-like power which all this induces is not illusory for, by the simple device of repeatedly jettisoning a teddy-bear or a rattle, any display of independence on the part of the mahout can successfully be countered, and should she, maddened beyond endurance, be provoked to reprisals a piteous howling will soon attract the friendly interest of sympathetic passers-by and expose her to public, if unjustified, rebuke. The gondola alone, I think, can compare with the pram for pleasure, but only on those occasions when one is certain that someone else will charge themselves with the nerve-racking financial dispute which will inevitably mark the journey's end.

In the far-off days before the first German war, travelling by pram in London was even more enjoyable than it is today: for on the few occasions that I accompanied my own children on their outings (though never being so foolish as to provide the motive power) I was much struck by the decline of street-life in the very districts which in my own childhood had been so packed with colour and incident. First, there was then an infinitely greater variety of traffic: classical milk-chariots driven by straw-hatted Ben-hurs (so much more exciting than the dreary little waggonettes of the present-day dairy combines), the even more dashing butcher's vans with the striped-aproned driver perched way aloft, the little painted donkey-carts of the costers who still wore their earrings and their high-waisted pearl-decorated jackets without the slight air of embarrassment natural to those making a hospital collection, emphasised and threw into strong relief the novelty of the occasional motor-vans. Secondly, the number of the street-traders and itinerant musicians had not yet been reduced to identical ranks of nylon-selling spivs and an occasional ex-service-men's band. There were innumerable Italian organ-grinders, male and female complete with monkey, and in those days Italians looked like Italians, all flashing teeth and curled moustaches—figures from *Cavalleria Rusticana*—not the slick dummies of the Coca-Cola lads of modern Italy: the Punch and Judy show was still a robust and common entertainment, not just a carefully pre-served survival of British folk-drama, and that high, ghastly cry, which familiarity never wholly robbed of its menace, was liable suddenly to startle at any street-corner: while the musical per-formers ranged all the way from the immensely dignified old lady who sang 'Just a Song at Twilight' to a harp accompaniment to the virtuoso who played the 'Light Cavalry Overture' on the musical glasses. Any knot of people at the kerb-side held a promise of entertainment, and the exact feel of the old forgotten excite-ment, so intimately bound up with memories of Kensington, returned to me once more when, many years later, a small crowd in the market-place of Argos parted to reveal a spectacle which until that moment I had never consciously remembered having seen before—a performing bear.

Even today Notting Hill Gate retains something of its original village atmosphere. Tucked away behind the intruding shopfronts, which in Victorian times encroached further and further on to the old Oxford road, eighteenth-century façades occasionally betray their presence by a cornice or a moulding projecting unexpectedly above the level of the black glass and chromium plate, recalling the district as a self-contained village.

In my pram-travelling days the old importance of the junction of the main road out of London to the West and the lane by the sandpits leading to Kensington had been recently reinforced by the opening of the Central London Tube immediately opposite the old Inner Circle station, but the resulting bustle and *va-et-vient* had still a local, almost provincial flavour, quite different to the anonymous big-city congestion of today. A crowd of prams, many of whose occupants were known to me personally, would at this hour be making the crossing towards the Gardens; other children's mothers or cooks would be emerging from the green-grocers or the lending-library; and a number of kindly old Colonels or cooing maiden-ladies would stop to make the usual jocular remark or to praise my exceptional beauty in terms that were none the less gratifying for being familiar.

But to these routine encounters had recently been added the possibility of far more exceptional and dramatic excitements. The women of Britain were on the march, and a crowd round the Post Office was a sure sign that they had recently demonstrated their political competence by heaving a brick through the window or pouring acid into the pillar-box. It never, unfortunately, fell to my lot to see a Suffragette but I was vividly aware of their existence. A close study of the press cartoons had taught me exactly what to look for and I habitually scanned every stretch of public railings hoping desperately for the sight of some grim-visaged, spectacled, hammer-waving Andromeda self-enchained. My light-hearted attitude to this vital question rather distressed my mother, a keen Shavian who at one time had moved in the progressive-minded circles centred on the Cobden Sanderson house in Chiswick Mall, but received every encouragement from Kate whose views accurately reflected the prevailing music-hall opinion and for whom Mrs. Pankhurst was as inexhaustible a source of amusement as were, at other times, such diverse public figures as Pussyfoot Johnson and Sydney Stanley.

Although invariably doomed in the matter of Suffragette outrages to arrive after the action was over, I was more fortunate in respect to street accidents—in those days more varied and less lethal. For some reason these seemed always to be concentrated in that stretch of the Bayswater Road between Notting Hill Gate and Queen's Road, and here I was, at various times, privileged to witness the collapse of a carthorse (and to retain for years to come the memory of the astonishingly light pink colour of the blood frothing from its mouth and nostrils, and the surprising number of passers-by eager and willing to sit traditionally on the poor animal's head), a white 'Arrow' omnibus bursting into flames, and to hear a deafening report which announced the head-on collision of two fast De Dion Boutons outside the chemist's. But best of all I enjoyed the sight, which remains vivid to this day, of a fashionable lady in a very tight hobble skirt of vivid purple falling flat on her face while running for an omnibus, a mishap provoking peals of happy, childish laughter all the way to the Round Pond.

Once past the old lady selling balloons—so much more disagreeable untransformed by the whimsical imagination of Sir James Barrie—and actually inside the Gardens which were the goal of our outing, my exultation was customarily transposed into a minor key. I was not as a child much attracted by the beauties of nature and keenly regretted the shops and street accidents thus temporarily abandoned, for which the expected encounters with little friends (governed as they were by the number of nannies with whom my own was at any particular moment on speaking terms) provided inadequate compensation. True, there was the Dutch Garden where nature was kept under proper control and the pleached limes formed tunnels of delight, and the Round Pond with its complement of miniature shipping, but here I was constantly disappointed by the lack of variety and was only buoyed up by the hope, seldom realised, of seeing a junk or a galleon, or even a three-masted schooner, anything in fact other than the inevitable

34

yachts which varied only in size. But chiefly was my rather jaundiced view of the Gardens coloured by the knowledge that sooner or later I should be forced to get out and walk, a development for which I could see no adequate justification, as even such an exceptional spectacle as workmen hanging fairy-lamps on the trees in celebration of the Coronation could be viewed just as well and in far greater comfort from the pram.

Our return route from the Gardens usually lay down the Queen's Road and Westbourne Grove, thoroughfares dominated and given character by the presence of Messrs. William Whiteley's emporium, an establishment which bulked very large in our family life. It is difficult nowadays to realise how very personal was then the relationship, even in London, between shop-keeper and customer and the enormous importance, comparable almost to that attained by rival churches, which late Victorian and Edwardian ladies attached to certain stores. All my female relatives had their own favourites, where some of them had been honoured customers for more than half a century and their arrival was greeted by frenzied bowing on the part of the frock-coated shopwalkers, and where certain of the older assistants stood to them almost in the relationship of confessors, receiving endless confidences on the state of their health, the behaviour of their pets and the general iniquity of the Liberal Government. Thus for my Great Aunt Bessie the Army and Navy Stores fulfilled all the functions of her husband's club and her undeviating loyalty was repaid by a respect and consideration which bore little or no relation to the size of her account. My mother's affections were chiefly centred on Harvey Nichols which her family had patronised for many years and which had been finally sanctified by her grandmother having met her death, at the age of ninety, at the wheels of a careless cyclist on leaving that establishment one summer morning in the last year of the old Queen's reign. However, although Harvey Nichols ever retained the first place in my mother's estimation, Knightsbridge was some way off and Queen's Road close at hand, so that Whiteley's had come to play the more important rôle. It was, moreover, already distinguished by being

35

the favourite shop of her aged Cousin Jenny who lived hard by in Inverness Terrace.

*   *   *   *   *

In a period still very rich in vintage old ladies Cousin Jenny was remarkable not so much for any individual quality (although by no means lacking in character) as for her completeness, as of some antique pot which was not, perhaps, at the time of its manufacture an outstanding masterpiece but which has been raised by the correctness of its silhouette, the fine preservation of its glaze and the perfection of its patina to the status of the supreme example of its type, providing the standard by which all other finds are graded. The only daughter of an enterprising Scotsman Douglas Lepraik, who had made a large fortune by introducing steam navigation on the Yangtse-Kiang, she had been destined for an important marriage. Unfortunately while still a girl in a finishing school in Brussels she had contracted small-pox of which the ravages had been so severe as to outweigh in the eyes of hoped-for aristocratic suitors the attraction of a handsome dot. She had eventually married, late in life by the standards of the period, one of her father's sea-captains who had quite recently died after many years of blissfully happy union; since when she had adopted a way of life as rigidly limited, but within its narrow confines as intense, as that of Proust's Tante Eulalie.

The house in Inverness Terrace, which provided so perfect a setting for the endlessly repeated cycle of Cousin Jenny's daily life, had been presented to her completely furnished by her father as a present on her wedding in the late 'seventies or early 'eighties and not the smallest alteration nor addition had since been made. There in the big bow window of the drawing-room, which commanded a good, clear view of the street in both directions, discreetly veiled by Nottingham lace curtains, she passed most of her waking life, protected from all possibility of draught by thick velvet *portières* and from interruption or assault by an immensely fat and disagreeable fox-terrier. Her principal occupation was the careful study of the *Morning Post* and this took a far greater time,

36

even given the much larger newspapers of those days, than one would have imagined. Not only did she read every word, including the stock prices (for she had inherited something of her father's shrewd Scots business sense), in itself a formidable task, but was forced to do so with only half an eye or in short snatches in order that no important development in the life of Inverness Terrace, such as the visit of the doctor to Number 8 or the progress of the promising romance between the parlour-maid at Number 11 and the new baker's roundsman, should escape her notice. Thus she was seldom more than half-way through her task when it was time for her only excursion, her daily visit to Whiteley's.

No abbess ever identified herself so closely with the life of her convent, nor any archaeologist with his 'dig', as did Cousin Jenny with that of Whiteley's Universal Stores. She had watched it grow from a small oil and paint shop to Sir Aston Webb's Renaissance Palazzo covering several acres; and while she would stoutly maintain in conversation with Great Aunt Bessie its manifest superiority to the Army and Navy Stores she had nevertheless invariably deplored all innovation and expansion and had foreseen nothing but future disaster arising from each successive change, from the abandonment of oil-lamps in favour of gas to the introduction of the soda-fountain. No incident was too trivial to hold her attention and the appearance of a new cashier in the hardware or a change in the colour of the parcel tape were immediately noted and gave rise to fears for the firm's stability hardly less grave than those aroused by the assassination of its original founder at the hands of an illegitimate son in the sweet department, an incident of which it was alleged she had been an eyewitness.

Cousin Jenny's daily outing invariably took place in the morning, so that by tea-time when visits from her family usually occurred she had been able to put in another two hours with the *Morning Post* and was completely master of what was for her the most important section, the Court Page. She was thus fully equipped to take the lead in the conversation, which could be sustained almost indefinitely, that was certain to arise whenever two or three of the older generation of my female relations were gathered together, about the doings, personalities and relationships of the Royal Family.

Was it not strange that the Queen of Spain had not come over to Kensington Palace this year, and did not that perhaps indicate that there would soon be another little grandchild for dear Princess Beatrice? How curious that one heard so little of Prince Albert of Schleswig-Holstein these days! Perhaps it was true that Queen Alexandra couldn't bear the sight of him and that was why he never went to Sandringham. Of course, one had always heard that his father had drunk like a fish and that sort of thing so often runs in families! Well, they would soon have to be looking round for a bride for the Prince of Wales, in a year or two's time he would be quite grown up. Of course there were always those Swedish princesses and one had heard talk of one of the Queen of Greece's girls. Anyhow one did hope that it would not be another of those Germans, always so plain and far too many of them in the family already!

In this style of *causerie* my aged cousin was an acknowledged virtuoso, sharply correcting any slip in the calculation of exact degrees of consanguinity, such as confusing a first cousin once removed with a second cousin, and displaying an astounding memory for the correct dates of births, marriages and accessions. Indeed for her one of the gravest inconveniences caused by the War when it came, worse than the rationing or the Zeppelin raids, was the difficulty it imposed in keeping fully posted on the activities of all Queen Victoria's German descendants. Although she lived on for many years, dying at a very advanced age in the early 'twenties, nothing in her way of life was ever changed (fortunately she did not live to see the disappearance of the *Morning Post*), and her strong personality remained unmodified to the end—or maybe even beyond, for it was at her funeral that for the only time in my life I came within measurable distance of what could be possibly described as a psychic phenomenon.

One of the ways in which Cousin Jenny's staunch unyielding conservatism had most strikingly expressed itself during her lifetime was in her firm refusal ever to contemplate the shortest journey in a horseless carriage and her continued use of a hired brougham for the regular visits to her banker and solicitor, the sole occasions on which she moved more than a stone's throw from the Queen's Road. Most inconsiderately those in charge of the *pompes funèbres* had ignored this idiosyncrasy and arranged for her to make her last journey in a motor-hearse. However, on the way to Kensal Rise this machine, a glittering and apparently perfectly functioning Rolls-Royce, broke down no less than three times and on the final occasion so completely that a substitute had hastily to be summoned by telephone. No sooner had Cousin Jenny been transferred to the new vehicle than this, too, began to develop engine-trouble, coming at last to a complete halt in the very gates of the cemetery, so that after further fruitless tinkering, the mutes were forced to shoulder the coffin for the good quarter of a mile to the mortuary chapel. After the service was over the by this time nearly hysterical mourners emerged to find the hearse once more standing ready, for from the moment it was relieved of its burden, the engine had responded perfectly. There still remained, however, the final lap to the grave itself at the furthest end of the cemetery and, with what I judged to be an ill-conceived determination, the undertakers once more transferred Cousin Jenny's mortal remains to the horseless carriage. Once more we all climbed into the attendant cars, once more the chauffeur swung the starting handle, once more there was absolutely no response. At last, the protesting mutes admitted defeat, and triumphantly reactionary, even in death, my aged cousin was borne to her final resting-place by man-power alone.

* * * * *

Once past William Whiteley's the homeward way lost much of its interest, for Westbourne Grove, although curiously enough still at that date quite a fashionable shopping street, had little enough in it at all times of the year, save one, to hold my attention and in retrospect is only remarkable for being the place where I saw my last horse-bus. The reason which formed the exception was the week or so immediately preceding Christmas when both kerb-sides were thick with toy-vendors selling the most extraordinary variety of novelties and play-things now only to be seen in the London Museum. Miniature 'knuts', who by the manipulation of a string could be made to bow and raise their top-hats revealing a great shock of golliwog hair; squads of wooden guardsmen that formed fours or line in obedience to the pressure exerted on the green painted trellis on which they were marshalled; toy goldfish swimming in what were apparently flashing globes of water but were in

reality simple loops of tin set spinning on a swivel: and, perhaps most remarkable of all, tiny Bibles the size of one's thumb-nail. "Li'l 'Oly Boible! Li'l 'Oly Boible! 'Orl the Good Book for tuppence!"

Although on week-days our return journey from the park had, save at Christmas time, a certain melancholy and sense of flatness, on Sundays the excitement was maintained to the very end. Our progress was then so timed as to bring us opposite St. John's, Notting Hill, at the hour at which my parents, along with the rest of the congregation, would emerge. For the present generation it is almost impossible to imagine how impressive a spectacle was the weekly Church Parade outside any one of a dozen or more London churches at the close of Morning Prayer on any fine Sunday in the early years of the century. At the moment of our arrival the street would be deserted save for one or two victorias and broughams at the church gates (never very many for, although the congregation contained a high proportion of 'carriage-folk', St. John's was rather Low and it was not thought right for any except the frail and aged to work their coachmen on the Sabbath), and the soft strains of Dykes would come floating out among the plane trees of Ladbroke Hill as the verger opened the doors at the final verse of the closing hymn. Then a short pause, a rustling murmur as the congregation rose from its knees gathering up prayer books and feather-boas and adjusting veils and gloves, and the first worshippers would emerge blinking a little in the bright sun pursued by the rolling chords of the voluntary. Soon the whole churchyard and street was a mass of elaborate, pale-shaded millinery, great cart-wheels à la Lily Elsie decorated with monstrous roses and doves in flight, old-fashioned bonnets trimmed with parma-violets, among which the glittering top-hats, ceaselessly doffed and replaced, provided the sharper, more definite accents.

Owing to the fact of my father, who was a churchwarden, being usually a little delayed by financial transactions in the vestry, I had ample opportunity to study and recognise the principal notables of our little world before my parents finally appeared. There was Sir Aston Webb, not yet president of the Royal Academy, cross-eyed and severe, resting on the seventh day from the labours of creating a new Buckingham Palace in the current Potsdam style; there was old Dr. Waldo, side-whiskered and benign, whose daughters I played with but the exact nature of whose functions as Chief Coroner for London no one would ever explain to me, albeit that the importance of this position was held to reflect great credit on the local community; there was Professor Perry who with his long hair, glasses and thick walrus moustache was the very type of the stage scientist, whose researches in electro-physics were nevertheless to bear abundant fruit in the coming war; and, at long last, there came my father.

The family reunion did not, however, by any means mark the end of the proceedings. Friends had to be greeted, enquiries made as to the progress of Old Mrs. So-and-So's cold, and views exchanged about the sermon. This last duty was more than purely nominal for at St. John's sermons were taken seriously and the congregation included many *cognoscenti* of fine preaching. The Vicar in my earliest childhood was a certain Canon, of whom only a vision of an angry red face remains to me as the children's service was invariably left to the Curate. Originally a fine preacher he had come of recent years increasingly to deviate from the path of strict orthodoxy, which had caused considerable dissension among his flock, so that his departure, which took place in circumstances sufficiently remarkable, was neither wholly unforeseen nor altogether regretted. In the course of one of his most rousing sermons, fortunately at Evensong, he announced that it had recently been revealed to him in a dream that there were no women in Heaven, the female part of mankind having finally been judged incapable of salvation. While those of his hearers who were acquainted with the Canon's wife could quite appreciate the obvious satisfaction with which the Vicar promulgated this new dogma, few among a congregation that was largely female could be expected to share it, and complaints to the Bishop led to the Canon's sudden retirement for a long rest in the country from which, in fact, he never returned.

In due course his place was taken by Canon Dudden, whose great reputation as a preacher and magnificent presence (he was, I think, at this time one of the most strikingly handsome men I ever remember seeing) made the appointment a very popular one with the congregation of St. John's. Whether it was equally gratifying to the Canon may be doubted, though this was not to be guessed at the time, for many years later when he once more, albeit distantly, entered my life as Vice-Chancellor of Oxford he was reported to be in the habit, when looking back on his career, of referring somewhat bitterly to "years of penance in the draughty parish-halls of North Kensington".

On most Sundays, if my behaviour had been thought to warrant

43

a treat, I now quitted my pram and accompanied my parents and the other churchwarden, old Colonel Hook, to the latter's house in the next street to ours for a pre-luncheon visit. Arrived, exhausted from the effort to keep up with the long strides of my companions, I would be plied with sweets and lemonade while they refreshed themselves with a whisky-and-soda. I would then be taken by the Colonel into his study where he would bring out for my benefit a series of military trophies culminating in his full-dress cocked hat which, if I were fortunate, I should be allowed to my immense satisfaction to try on.

Of all the extraordinary interiors of my childhood, of which the atmosphere has been rendered by subsequent events remote from all modern experience, the most difficult to convey to any reader under forty-five was Colonel Hook's study. The faded sepia ranks of brother-officers, moustachioed, whiskered, bearded, staring straight ahead from under the peaks of monstrously high topees or jaunty little pill-boxes, their gloved hands clasped on chased sword-hilts, the water-colour sketches of forgotten cantonments with long rows of bell-tents and skeletal pyramids of stacked rifles, the yellowing maps with little coloured oblongs marking the spot where the Company made their last stand and the route taken by the relieving column indicated by a straggling procession of beetle-like arrows, the knobkerries, the assegais, the Pathan knives—all spoke of a way of military life as far removed from that with which we are familiar as that of the Roman legions. For Colonel Hook belonged entirely to the world of Lady Butler and Sir Henry Newbolt, of thin red lines and broken squares, of stockades and fuzzy-wuzzies, and displayed all its very real virtues in the highest degree. Although a little bent by the years his figure, in the short-tailed old-fashioned cut-away he usually wore, remained unmis-takably military; his Roman nose, thick brows and long walrus moustache combined with the high white collar to make him the very image of the fictional colonel. However, of the traditional failings of the type he was completely free, being extremely gentle in manner and the reverse of peppery so that it was quite as impossible to picture him ever losing his temper as it was to imagine that he could under any circumstances break his word. His whole life had centred round a single-minded devotion to his regiment and he could not conceive it possible that any man could ask for a more rewarding career than the army.

Even as he had lived it Colonel Hook's life, and that of all those whiskered captains, had been, one can now see, anachronistic. It was, at this date, some fifty years since General Sherman had ravaged Georgia (the full significance of which event seems at the time to have escaped the notice of almost everyone save Napoleon III), and yet here we all were, grown-ups just as vividly as little boys, on the very eve of disaster, still envisaging war in terms of bugle-calls and charging lancers. So ridiculous does this now seem to us that we tend in retrospect to dismiss all these little colonial wars as playing at soldiers and denigrate by implication the heroism and courage of Colonel Hook and his like. What they had been spared was the realisation which only came gradually even after 1914, of the immense gravity attaching to the outcome of the fight, the large-scale anxiety transcending the personal which must lie at the back of any modern mind, however much it may be deliberately or unconsciously suppressed in action. If the relieving column did not arrive, or the ammunition run out so much the worse for the regiment; it was unthinkable, so accustomed to victory was that generation, that the ultimate outcome of the campaign would be affected. And even if by some extraordinary and terrible turn of events, or an act of betrayal on the part of Liberal politicians, the war itself should be lost, no threat to the British way of life would result; a whole battalion might be wiped out, national prestige sadly dimmed, but not a penny more would go on the income-tax, the Derby would still be run, and silk hats and frock-coats would still be worn at church parade.

＊　　＊　　＊　　＊　　＊

When the storm finally broke which blew Colonel Hook and all his paladins way down the corridor of history, I was at the seaside. Each summer at the beginning of August I was sent with my nurse to an admirable boarding-house kept by an old governess of my

45

father's at Littlehampton, where in due course I would be joined by my parents. The unbutlined Littlehampton of those days represented the English seaside at its best. Separated from the sea by a wide expanse of green, rows of bow-fronted Regency villas looked across the channel; on the sands pierrots, nigger minstrels, and on Sundays Evangelical Missioners, provided simple entertainment for those who had temporarily exhausted the delights of digging, paddling and donkey rides; there was even a charming little harbour with shipyards on the Arun which ran into the sea alongside a severely-functional jetty raised by the presence of two slot-machines and some wooden benches to the dignity of a 'Pier' in the local esteem. So over-exciting did the atmosphere here normally prove—the heady smell of low-tide in the harbour, the salty taste on the back of one's hands, the feel of the firm sand under bare feet—that even had our arrival not preceded my birthday on the 4th by so short a space, I should have had little attention to spare for current events. It did, however, strike me as I waited at the station on the morning of the third for my mother, that the crowd meeting the London train was, perhaps, larger and more restless than usual; that the paper-sellers alongside large posters depicting figures wearing what appeared to be rather high bowlers decorated with cocks-plumes above the legend in purple type 'Gallant Little Belgium', were doing a brisker trade than usual. But as I had no idea as to who on earth the Belgians were I not unnaturally attributed the increased public excitement to a general awareness that tomorrow was my birthday. I did notice, however, that my mother when she arrived seemed more preoccupied than usual and answered my nurse's enquiries in that irritatingly swift low-pitched tone reserved by grown-ups for the discussion of matters declared to be 'above my head'. As a result I was instantly seized by a ghastly fear that my birthday present had been forgotten or mislaid.

Very early the next morning my fears proved groundless and the excitement produced by opening parcels, trying out a new pistol and aligning rows of topeed riflemen (the very spit and image of those commanded by Colonel Hook) in the correct formation for receiving the charge of an equal number of naked Zulus emerging from a grove of tastefully displayed tin palm-trees, lasted sufficiently long to prevent my remarking any untoward seriousness in the dining-room at breakfast. Moreover, my father had come down late the night before and the prospect of his company for a whole long morning on the sands was quite sufficient to engage my whole attention.

And yet the beach when we got there did seem subtly different. The number of long-legged little girls in floppy *broderie anglaise* sunhats (the exact look of whom against the sea and sand has been so perfectly recorded for all time in the very early paintings of Wilson Steer) was not visibly reduced, most of my accustomed playmates and their nannies were there, and only the grown-ups and casual strollers seemed fewer than usual. In what then did this sense of the unusual lie? At last I discovered what was wrong; my favourite among all the beach entertainers—a small brass-band composed of rather plump elderly gentlemen with long hair and thick glasses clad rather improbably in tight-braided hussar uniforms, who would normally at this hour be giving a spirited rendering of a selection from *Tannhauser* two breakwaters away from our hut— were nowhere to be seen. After fruitless searching up and down the length of the beach, in which I accounted for the presence of the ice-cream seller, the pierrots, the donkey boy, I finally put the problem to my father who was lying flat on his back on the shingle with his panama tilted over his eyes. The only reply I got was the whistled refrain of a familiar popular tune—

"Has anyone seen a *Ger*man band,
"*Ger*man band,
"*Ger*man band,
"I've looked everywhere both *near* and far,
"*Near* and far,
"*Ja*, Ja, Ja,
"But I miss my Fritz
"What plays twiddley-bits
"On the big trombone."

3. "My little grey home in the West"

FROM THE TOP of the omnibus the cloudless sky over-
arching the parallel uniformities of Redcliffe Gardens seemed
both bluer and more immediate than from street-level. It
was, indeed, one of the many advantages of the old open-deckers
that on them one enjoyed a sense of spaciousness, an awareness of
immensity, that has almost vanished from our modern urban life
approximating ever more closely to the central-heated ideal of
inter-communicating *machines-à-habiter*. As a child I was always,
therefore, exceptionally conscious of the heavens above when
riding on omnibuses, but on this particular Sunday afternoon my
attention had been concentrated and rendered more intense by

49

the fact that my fellow-passengers, as well as the passers-by on the flanking pavements, were one and all steadfastly scanning the brilliant strip of light South Kensington azure immediately above their heads. What I expected to see, I have no idea; a flight of wild swans, perhaps, or a belated competitor in the Gordon-Bennett balloon race. For what at length, my wondering gaze excitedly directed by my father, I saw, I could hardly have been more unprepared.

No one, who was so keen a reader of the *Illustrated London News* as I was, could possibly have remained ignorant of the existence of heavier-than-air craft, even if, unlike me, they had not been collectors of cigarette-cards, or been taken on so many fruitless expeditions to Wormwood Scrubs on the chance of seeing Mr. Graham White and his new flying-machine; nevertheless, the sudden spectacle of the fantastic, open-work reality elegantly suspended no great distance above the romantic towers of Mr. Waterhouse's museum, the sun gleaming through the oiled silk of the wings, a pair of bicycle wheels clearly visible beneath, afforded me one of the most powerful visual sensations of my whole childhood. That the passage immediately above our heads of a daring aeronaut should have thrown me, at the age I was in 1913, into a state of almost uncontrollable excitement was hardly surprising: that my father, who had frequently seen such sights before, should have been almost equally affected, and to a far greater degree than any other of our fellow-passengers, was less to be expected. The reason, which was revealed by the information he almost immediately imparted, was not at the time apparent to me. The aeroplane, he explained, was a 'Taube', which meant in German 'a dove', and was so called from the peculiar shape of the wings. My father, whose knowledge of Germany was first-hand and extensive, must in fact have been asking himself the question which was to vex so many leader-writers in the next few days. What was a German military flying-machine doing over London at so remarkably low a level on a brilliant Sunday afternoon in the summer of 1913?

Even when not rendered memorable by the incidence of the first

50

swallow of the Luftwaffe, my regular expeditions to visit my grand-father on Putney Hill were always enjoyable, anyhow in part. For one thing I was frequently accompanied by my father, of whom I saw little during the week, and in whose company I delighted; for another, they always involved a ride on a bus. This latter circumstance was less welcome to my father than to me, for he had inherited to the full the Lancaster passion for healthy exercise, which unaccountably did not, in my case, survive a further generation, and he was usually accustomed on these occasions to walk the whole distance from Kensington to Putney and back. This was manifestly impossible when I was of the party, and so the greater part of the distance was then covered by omnibus. For only when some member of the family was recovering from illness, or the weather quite exceptionally inclement, did my grandfather consent to send either a carriage or the motor-car. This omission, which in no way sprang from any meanness of character, was in part due to the fact that our visits usually took place on a Sunday, and in my grandfather's house the Biblical injunctions on the Sabbath employment of men-servants and maid-servants still retained much of their force, and due even more, I fancy, to a fear which never left a true Lancaster lest any such trouble-saving gesture would encourage a 'softening' process against which he must always be on guard, both in himself and others. Indeed, the omnibus itself was considered an indulgence but partly justified by my short legs and tender years, and was only tolerated on the understanding that I was to get out at Putney station and walk up the hill.

This to me intolerably long ascent was seldom, when accom-panied by Lancaster relations other than my father, accomplished without frequent bickering and occasional tears, for my constant complaints of exhaustion were not only invariably disregarded but often provoked speculations which seemed to me uncalled for and irrelevant. What, I was asked, would I do were I in the army? Or how should I get on in the company of Captain Scott? In vain did I pant out that I had no intention of going into the army (in those halcyon days such assurance on the part of small boys was not seemingly unduly optimistic), still less of taking part in any expeditions to the Antarctic: all such protests were brushed aside as purely superficial and in no way affecting the principle at stake. Today, however, my father was with me and all was well, for not only did his conversation successfully dispel the boredom which this particular thoroughfare normally produced, but even had I felt tired I should in his company have made every effort to conceal the fact.

At that date my chief complaint against Putney Hill was the total absence of shops, for the fascinating vagaries of Victorian domestic architecture did not have for me the charm and interest which later they came to exercise, and its immense residential dullness was only occasionally relieved by a steam omnibus bursting into flames on approaching the summit, or the spectacle of my Uncle Jack with a coach-top full of my cousins driving his four-in-hand back to Wimbledon. Even the possibility of being kissed by Mr. Swinburne on his daily round from No. 2 The Pines to *The Green Man* on the heath had recently been removed by the great poet's death.

(Nevertheless I have always claimed, and shall continue to do so, that this honour was vouchsafed me at an age so tender as to be beyond the reach of memory, on the perfectly reasonable grounds that it is *just* chronologically possible, and, seeing that he kissed almost every small child he passed, including all my cousins who were noticeably less attractive than I was, it is highly unlikely that I should have been missed out when so frequently in the neighbourhood.)

Normally by the time we had reached the top all the petty diversions—such as counting the number of houses with names as opposed to those with numbers, or deliberately treading on dog's-mess in order to provoke my nurse or my aunt, or scuffling my new white shoes in the dead leaves in the gutter—had long since been exhausted, and the vision of my grandfather's house was greeted by me with an enthusiasm considerably greater than either its intrinsic beauty or the social delights there awaiting me would seem to have justified.

'South Lynn', as it was called, was a large four-square Victorian

mansion in yellow brick set well back from the road behind a
semi-circular drive encompassing a circle of superlatively well-kept
lawn adorned with a flag-pole. To the right as one approached
was a stable-yard with a glazed roof which was rendered chiefly
remarkable for me by the branch of a tree which Mundy, the

coachman, there preserved, nailed alongside the garage door,
from the appearance of which he was able to forecast the weather
with remarkable accuracy. In the centre of the façade was an
imposing front door approached by a flight of white marble steps
of so lethal a slipperiness that they were each separately furnished
with a little rubber mat, and flanked by a pair of stained glass
damsels clutching sunflowers and dressed in the Burne-Jones taste,
through which, having swung expectantly on the wrought-iron

bell-pull, I was accustomed to peer in order to catch the first fuzzy glimpse of the approaching parlourmaid's white cap and apron.

On entering the hall the thing of which I was always immediately conscious, as in any house other than our own, was the smell. Is smell the first of the senses to atrophy, or have the rich individual smells of forty years ago fallen victim, along with so much else, to the hygienic standardisation of the age? Certainly the houses and places of my childhood seem in retrospect to have been far more richly endowed in this respect than they are today. Even the mingled flavour of 'caporals', garlic and cheap Belgian coal, which was formerly far more evocative of Paris than the sight of the Arc-de-Triomphe or even the sound of taxi horns in the night, seemed on my last visit far fainter than formerly, while no nostrils under thirty-five could now possibly recognise, in the unlikely event of their ever encountering it, that extraordinary mixture of hot tar, horse-dung and lime trees which to me in my childhood spelt London in the early summer.

The peculiar smell of South Lynn, now unrecallable but instantly to be detected—a subtle mingling of Havana cigars and Knight's Castile soap—although general in all the houses of my Lancaster relatives, was as different as possible from that prevailing in my other grandfather's house, and instantly set in motion a whole related train of ideas and reactions, so that had it ever happened by some supernatural fluke that the smells of the one house should have greeted me on entering the other, I should have been as hopelessly at sea as one of Professor Pavlov's dogs for whom the wrong bell has tolled.

Quite apart from its smell, the hall was remarkable enough and in the highest degree characteristic of my grandfather and his way of life. Immediately facing one on entering, a broad flight of stairs rose to the darkness of a half-landing; balustered in polished oak they ended in a newel post surmounted by a carved figure in vaguely mediaeval costume holding aloft an electric *flambeau* with the red rose of Lancaster blazoned in colour on his surcoat. The walls between massively architectural oak doors leading to other rooms were adorned by a series of portraits of ladies and gentlemen in the wigs and stomachers of Queen Anne's day, reputedly ancestral, in whose features the more credulous of my relations, such as my mother, were constantly detecting striking resemblances to existing aunts and uncles, but whose connection with the family the more sceptical were occasionally heard to describe, when sagely out of earshot of my grandfather, as tenuous. Even I, as romantic and uncritical a child as ever thumbed through Burke, was never able to work out quite to my satisfaction exactly how a seventeenth-century worthy, wearing what appeared to be the robes of an Elector of the Holy Roman Empire, was to be fitted in to our not over-glamorous family tree. Further to emphasise, although perhaps a little confusedly, the prevailing atmosphere of antiquity, the space immediately above the drawing-room door had been tastefully adorned with a suit of Arab chain-mail, a mediaeval helmet and a couple of scimitars, the whole achievement being underlined, as it were, by a Zulu knobkerrie brought back from Africa by an uncle who had served in the Boer war.

The drawing-room, into which on these occasions we were immediately shown, always seemed enormous. Even allowing for the notorious enlargement effected by the eye of memory, it must, I think, have been an extensive apartment in order to have accommodated the quite extraordinarily large quantity of furniture without ever appearing over-crowded. In addition to the usual complement of chintz-covered sofas and armchairs and a concert grand, there were enough occasional tables, china cabinets, escritoires, bureaux, pouffes, side-tables, ottomans and footstools to have furnished a Cunarder. These pieces—mainly in rosewood or satinwood—it was obvious did not exist for themselves alone but rather for the functional purpose of providing a resting-ground for an enormous population of china, ivory and bronze figures which my grandfather had brought back, chained to his chariot-wheels, from his regular triumphant tours of foreign parts. The mantelpiece, draped in green velvet, harboured a quantity of eighteenth-century gods and goddesses, whose amorous abandon and equivocal attitudes could only be justified by their being Dresden of the best period. In the china cabinet were further witnesses to the affection which that city always inspired in the Lancaster family, not so valuable perhaps, but less embarrassing; dainty rogues in porcelain whose clothes, meticulously rendered with every lace frill standing out in neurasthenic detail, were indeed of eighteenth-century cut but whose simpering expressions and arch posturing proclaimed them natives of that Victorian version of the Georgian age—all candlelight, sedan-chairs and "Fie, Lady Betty", the world in fact of Lewis Waller in *Monsieur Beaucaire*—which found its fullest expression in the works of Marcus Stone and Dendy Sadler, and which has today been happily perpetuated by the producers of Hollywood.

Hardly less numerous than the porcelain beaux and belles, and even more astounding in their realistic rendering of detail, were the ivories. Japanese peasants carrying bundles of wood in which every branch and twig was separately and convincingly carved: pot-bellied sages the size of one's thumbnail: geishas whose elaborately pleated and embroidered robes were in striking contrast to the expressionless formality of their faces. My favourite in this collection, however, was not oriental, but a bust of Mary Queen of Scots whose bosom opened to reveal the whole scene of her execution complete with clergyman, headsman and weeping attendants, contained in the space of her lungs. The bronze population was of less interest, for the intractable nature of the material did not allow of such detailed modelling, and for me, as for all normal children, it was detail that counted. Indeed, I can only recall, out of all that dusky host, a Moroccan runner carrying the good news from Fez to Rabat and a melancholy Zouave resting on a rocky promontory.

But these studies from life were not by any means the sole witnesses to my family's familiarity with foreign culture. In addition there were several reproductions carried out in low relief in marble and gilding of the arcading of the Alhambra, framed and backed with red velvet; an alabaster model of the Tower of Pisa, and several large plates bearing hand-painted views of the Royal Palace at Stockholm; and a really very fine bronze model of the equestrian statue of Marcus Aurelius on the Campodoglio.

Curiously enough, the innumerable water-colours on the surrounding walls, though less exotic in subject-matter than the marshalled rows of *Reise-andenken,* came far closer to being works of art. A river-scene by David Cox, a view of Antwerp by Prout, several interiors of Italian Palaces, an anonymous drawing of the Boston Stump and a number of Birkett-Fosters reflected a taste that even then was old-fashioned and has not yet come back again into favour, but which was nevertheless genuine.

In appearance my grandfather, for whom this whole crowded scene existed to provide a background, was at this time, and indeed remained until his death at an advanced age many years later, one of the most completely realised personalities on whom I have ever set eyes. A tall, big man, he did not give the impression of great height owing largely to the size of his head, which was enormous, square and completely, shinily bald; but for the austerity conditions prevailing above the line of the ears he had been richly, perhaps over-compensated on a lower-level. Beneath immensely thick brows, jutting out like cornices, were just visible a pair of extremely bright hazel eyes, a determined nose, roman-esque rather than Roman, and two round and polished cheeks, thrusting up like twin tumuli from a hawthorn thicket. And that was all. From immediately below the nostrils right down to the navel there cascaded a snow-white beard of that particular strength and thickness only achieved by those who have never in their life employed a razor. The general effect was one of extreme benevo-lence, but nevertheless one was conscious that Father Christmas could, if necessary, double the part of Jove. This awareness of latent strength, which certainly justified the nervous awe which tempered the affectionate regard in which his whole family held him, was partly due, I think, to the slightly enigmatic expression—so marked in Moslem women—of those whose mouths are always hidden. For contrary to popular belief the mouth is a far more revealing feature than the eyes, and in my grandfather's case I constantly found myself speculating as to its exact size and shape, and whether it supported or contradicted the impression of warm-hearted joviality which the visible part of his countenance

57

established. Was it perpetually wreathed in laughing curves, as one would at first sight assume, or was it set in a firm determined line as his reputation and career might have suggested? No one could tell me for by this time no man living had ever seen it; but, curiously enough, the only available evidence, a childhood portrait, indicated that it was, or once had been, delicately curved and rather feminine.

The greeting which I received never varied; after prolonged chuckling, as though my appearance recalled some side-splitting joke temporarily forgotten, my grandfather always made the same announcement which dated, I fancy, from my first visit in some early sailor-suit, " 'Pon my word, ain't he a howlin' swell!"

Having smirked embarrassedly at this familiar sally, I dived into the undergrowth and planted a kiss in what I hoped was the general direction of his cheek, after which I respectfully saluted whatever aunts happened to be present in the same manner. These formalities over, there came, if it were summer, the expected, and by me not over-enthusiastically received, feminine proposal, "Well, I think we've just time for a little run in the garden before tea."

Although never as a child a friend to violent exercise, I would not have it thought that I was so incurably soft as not to be able to face a gentle turn round an ordinary suburban garden; but this was not an ordinary suburban garden, and the phrase 'a little run' in the Lancastrian usage had sinister implications. First we passed through a conservatory attached at right angles to the drawing-room, which was in itself a source of frustration for I would gladly have lingered for longer than I was ever given a chance to do in an apartment which for me was always steeped in a curious, jungle romance. Around a tiled pool, in which two depressed golden carp of immense size circulated among improbable conch-shells, there flourished palms and giant ferns and banks of potted lobelias and calceolarias beneath a glazed sky barely visible through a tangle of maiden-hair.

All my life I have retained a deep affection for conservatories. To have gathered and selected all the more strikingly unfamiliar plant-forms, many of them sounding overtones of the highest

59

romance—of oases, of desert islands, of the Promenade des Anglais —behind glass walls through which the reality of Nature with all its untidiness, insects and dirt is clearly visible, and further, as here, to have reinforced this Douanier Rousseau-like treatment of the jungle with the addition of water and fish which are themselves a living testimony to the transforming power of art, has always seemed among our most civilised achievements. Unfortunately, although my enthusiasm was in no way shared by my aunts, they must, I fancy, have guessed at it, and classed it as unhealthy—part and parcel in fact of little Osbert's tendency to 'softness'—against which they waged so incessant and disinterested a warfare; and we always descended the iron stairs to the garden with a noticeable briskness.

As it was a Sunday, and anyhow I was still considered too young, the risk of being involved in a game of tennis was not yet serious, and the only danger I had to fear in this upper part of the garden was that of inadvertently treading on the grass edges of the lawn. The reaction which this mishap always produced in my grandfather was immediate and terrifying; indeed, his outbursts if the risk of any damage to his lawns (which invariably met the surface of the gravel in a right-angled turn as sharp and clean-cut as any architectural moulding) was imminent, were the only signs of rage I ever saw him exhibit, and so lent colour to the view which I had frequently heard expressed, but should otherwise have found difficult to credit, that "your grandfather can be very terrible when roused".

From the upper garden we descended by a flight of Italianate balustraded steps flanked with geraniums in urns to a region of flower and vegetable beds. The time spent here depended very largely on whether there were any little tasks at which it was thought I could usefully assist. If there were no sweet-peas to be cut, or green-fly to be sprayed, or, worst of all, some patch which the gardener's boy had neglected properly to weed, the whole party passed admiringly but swiftly to the greenhouses, my grand-father's especial pride. Here in the dry, clean heat hung row upon row of slowly ripening, still translucent, grapes which would later be cut down and distributed round the various Lancaster households. But never, alas, in quite the quantity which their present abundance would seem to warrant, for despite this encouraging display the patriarchal vines never completely fulfilled their early promise. The fact was, of course, that my grandfather, like so many men who have justly acquired a great reputation as shrewd judges of character, impossible to hoodwink, was always taken in by his gardener who habitually reserved a sizeable proportion of the crop for private sale to the greengrocer down the road.

Beyond the greenhouses lay a coach-house and a yard in which a sheepdog of demonstrative friendliness but appalling smell was kennelled, and here, were it not for 'The Field', the garden would have ended.

'The Field', which was separated from the main garden by a still surprisingly rural lane, was, curiously enough, all that the same implied. Roughly oval in shape and bordered by elms, through the branches of which the roofs of the villas in Putney Vale were only just visible, it sloped down to a pond and a rustic summerhouse diagonally across from the gate in the lane. Despite the summerhouse and the villas it fulfilled many of the functions of a proper country field, bearing an annual crop of hay and from time to time witnessing church fêtes and school sports, and its apparent size cannot have been wholly illusory as it is today covered by a housing estate. Nevertheless, apart from a snobbish satisfaction that my grandfather's demesne was thereby rendered so much more extensive than his neighbours', the feelings which the existence of this unexpected *pleasaunce* aroused in me were mixed: it was, except in the immediate vicinity of the pond, quite unromantic and its bleak open spaces afforded far too many opportunities for violent exercise. Indeed, my worst fears were usually confirmed immediately on entering by the spectacle of a band of cousins already engaged in a heavily organised game of rounders, tiny gesticulating figures, all black stockings and *broderie anglaise*, silhouetted against the yellowish green of the grass, away in the middle distance.

My childish reluctance to involve myself in violent sport, which

61

I have but partially overcome in later life, did not spring, as my aunts thought, so much from congenital laziness as from causes which, from the moral point of view, were hardly less censurable— a vanity which robbed of pleasure almost all occupations at which I was unable to shine, and a sad lack of the 'team spirit'. Added to these was a natural garrulity which, for reasons that I have never fully understood, was always firmly checked in the interests of 'playing the game'. Of this, years have not brought understanding, and I remain of the opinion that there is no game from bridge to cricket that is not improved by a little light conversation; a view which, I discovered in my pilgrimage from prep school to University, is shared only by a small and unjustly despised minority.

In the Lancaster family, games were not considered as suitable opportunities for individual self-expression and were invariably strictly supervised, and while failure to shine was never allowed to pass without jocular comment, success, in view of the danger of 'getting a swollen head', was always passed over in silence, or greeted in such a way that the victor was left in no doubt that his triumph was either undeserved or could easily have been surpassed had he but exerted himself a little more. The appearance of a housemaid at the gate of the field announcing tea was ready was, therefore, always a welcome sight despite the fact the grown-up in charge had invariably, with an infinite cunning, so arranged matters that the whole party were by this time at the extreme low bottom of the field and the ensuing race back to the house, from which there was no escape and in which I would inevitably come in an inglorious last easily outdistanced both by those who were younger and by those of gentler sex, was thereby stretched to its uphill maximum.

Of all the rooms in my grandfather's house, the dining-room where we finally ended up, panting and vaguely ashamed, has left the deepest impression. This was in no way the result of any super- lative excellence of the meals there consumed, for the Lancasters had no understanding, and but very limited appreciation, of food (their ideal of a gastronomic paradise was one where cold roast mutton appeared at every meal and the cook, a vile-tempered

62

Devonshire woman, would have earned unfavourable comment in a British Railways hotel). It was rather the decoration, and prevailing atmosphere of immeasurable solidity, which made it memorable. On the walls pictures were ranged so thick it was impossible to get any clear idea of the exact pattern of the tooled and stamped wallpaper in the fractional spaces left between the heavy gold frames; pictures chiefly of storms at sea, blasted heaths and gloomy woods to many of which had been attached, rather optimistically as it was later to turn out, such names as Van der Velde and Old Crome. The only bright spots among the menacing storm-clouds and angry seas were provided by two portraits, one of my grandfather in mayoral robes, the other of an uncle in full regimentals.

The room, which ran almost the whole depth of the house, divided itself into sections on either side of the door. That to the left, already rendered menacing by the presence of a concentration of all the stormier works of art, was made still more sombre by the fact that its only source of illumination was a window which, as it looked out on to the stable-yard, was enriched by stained glass in the style of Walter Crane: that to the right was more cheerful not only thanks to the presence of the military uncle but also to a large bow-window in which stood a bronze tripod copied from the one in the Naples Museum (with, in so far as the more virile aspect of the supporting satyrs was concerned, rather less than a painstaking fidelity) and which was always gay with hothouse plants. On an extraordinary chest, carved in high relief by a well-known A.R.A. with frenzied mediaeval joustings, was kept the greatest of the room's treasures. In an elaborately chased gold casket decorated in a style which nicely combined a proper awareness of civic antiquity with an up-to-date acquaintance with the vagaries of art-nouveau in its more readily accepted academic form, enriched with enamel plaques bearing views of the town of which the painstaking realism would, in another setting, have taken on some of the quality of coloured post-cards, lay the Freedom of King's Lynn, presented to my grandfather at an impressive ceremony some years earlier.

Of all the numberless teas, luncheons, and dinners which I consumed in that gloomy apartment only a vague generalised memory remains. The food never varied, the well-named rock-cakes, the 'shapes' presumably so called because they had no other attribute, a peculiarly nauseating cocoa-flavoured rice-pudding, along with the inevitable cold mutton and excellent Stilton made their regular appearance year after year. Just as familiar were the faces of those around the table for, save for occasional dinner-parties to city friends which had practically come to an end for lack of contemporaries by the time I was of an age to attend them, my grandfather was unaccustomed to extend his hospitality much beyond the family circle. Even then the range was more limited than it need have been, for at any given moment my unmarried aunts were certain not to be on speaking terms with at least two of their sisters-in-law. It was only under the pressure of a European war that any noticeable extension was affected.

I have frequently thought that the coming of the Belgian refugees in 1914, and the resultant clash of cultures, provides one of the most psychologically rewarding, and strangely neglected, themes for which any dramatist or novelist could ask. For at that time not only were the English middle classes, who received the major proportion, far more insular than they are today—in the average household no member, save perhaps a daughter who had 'finished' in Paris, was likely ever to have exchanged a word with a foreigner, apart from the porters, customs-officials and guides encountered on conducted tours—but the whole conception of the refugee, now of so melancholy a familiarity, was utterly new and startling. How many fantastic encounters, inevitable readjustments and strange awakenings, one wonders, resulted from this brief incursion?

In my grandfather's case two circumstances combined to render the situation more than normally fantastic. His family had not indeed been isolated from continental experience so rigidly as most, but as their foreign contacts had been exclusively German, in which country most of them had finished their education, this was naturally most productive of awkward pauses and hasty rephrasings. And, as I now recognise, they had been subject to a peculiar time-lag which rendered their way of life strangely old-fashioned and caused them staunchly to uphold values which even in their native land had been called in question at least a quarter of a century before.

Of the two bewildered Belgian families who found an asylum at South Lynn the first was the more colourful, the second the more interesting, and in my case, as things turned out, rewarding. Commandant Kroll and his wife impressed themselves on my memory partly by his uniform (how strange in the eyes of childhood is the first sight of a uniform, normally associated with guardsmen, policemen and other hieratic and unreal figures of the outside world, when worn indoors!), but even more by the strange nature of the mortifications which wounded patriotism caused them to inflict on themselves. Mme Kroll's refusal, frequently announced, to wear her wedding-ring so long as a single German remained on Belgian soil was, to my mind, illogical rather than spectacular, but her husband's resolution to refrain from dying his purple-black moustaches for a similar period produced a result, anyhow in the early days, gratifyingly piebald and bizarre. However, apart from the Commandant's persistent efforts, vaguely resented, to cut up my meat for me at table, my relations with this monolingual pair remained distant. And anyhow they soon vanished after a dramatic scene, involving enraged stepsons, waved revolvers and passionate behaviour all round, that confirmed my family in their worst suspicions about Continental home-life.

Very different were the Van den Eckhoudts who succeeded the Krolls. Although, as I only came to realise many years later, their way of life was possibly even further removed, albeit in a totally different direction, from that of their hosts, there soon developed a mutual regard warming to affection which far outlasted the period of exile. Monsieur 'Van den', as he came to be called, was burdened by the grave disadvantage, in the eyes of his hosts, of be-ing a painter; and, moreover, not one who had been driven into that employment by force of circumstance but who had deliberately

chosen it in preference to what would doubtless have been a highly profitable, and from the Lancastrian viewpoint eminently praiseworthy, business career open to him as the son of a wealthy Brussels banker. To make matters still worse it soon became apparent that his work, upon which he immediately engaged, bore little or no resemblance to that of dear old Mr. Roe, the brother of the Rector of St. Nicholas at Lynn, whose colourful presentation of such scenes as 'Nelson on the bridge of the Victory' or 'The Old Chelsea Pensioner' had recently gained for him an A.R.A. and many of whose masterpieces, including the Mayoral portrait and the mediaeval chest, were scattered round the house. M. Van den was, in fact, a modern painter; and unfortunately the scandal of the First Post-Impressionist Exhibition had been so heavily publicised that even a household as utterly cut off from all contact with contemporary art as was South Lynn had by now been made fully aware of its appalling implications.

The slight nervousness which the nature of M. Van den's occupation induced in my aunts—reinforced as it was by the unfortunate incident of the Krolls—while it could not possibly, in face of his extreme gentleness of manner (his appearance with his large features and rich mane of hair suggested the attempt of some archaic sculptor only acquainted with sheep to achieve a lion by hearsay) and the charm and evident good nature of his remarkably handsome wife, amount to anything as strong as antagonism, did at first make for a certain restraint which, curiously enough, worked ultimately to my great advantage. For my mother, alone of the whole Lancaster clan, had had personal experience of the artist's life, and her sympathy with modern painting was considerably greater than the fact that she was a pupil of the late G. F. Watts might have suggested. She had, moreover, been educated in Brussels and worked for a time in the studio of a master under whom M. Van den had himself studied, and she it was who provided him with the tools of his trade, lost with all the rest of his luggage on the flight, and constituted herself the champion of his work in all family discussions. In this she was undoubtedly actuated by a genuine admiration, for it was obvious

67

to all who were not blinded by the unaccustomed lightness of his palette and a very restrained simplification of form, that M. Van den was an artist of the greatest sensibility and accomplishment, but almost certainly her defence derived an additional zest from the opportunity it afforded of, for once, putting her sisters-in-law in the wrong.

It was natural, therefore, that our household should have seen rather more of the Van dens than did the other branches of the family: with the fortunate sequel, some fifteen years later, that it was to their home, by then removed to Roquebrune, that I was sent to learn French. It was only at this later period that I was able fully to realise how extraordinary a transposition their sojourn on Putney Hill must in fact have been, and to gain, from their reminiscences, a completely detached and unengaged picture of my grandfather and his way of life.

The Van dens' household in the South of France when first I visited it in the late 'twenties, a callow but absorbent under-graduate, proved the gateway to a world of which, until that time, I had been ignorant of the very existence. The villa itself, 'La Couala', very white and simple, seemed by contrast with home bare and under-furnished. Even the books which stretched from floor to ceiling on plain unvarnished shelves looked in their yellow or white paper naked and temporary, while the austere peasant-made chairs and tables seemed but the frames of furniture still awaiting their padding and chintz. Only the grand piano had a vaguely familiar look which did not, however, extend to the music-rest, for the works there lying open were signed not by Amy Woodforde-Findon or Sir Arthur Sullivan, but such unknown personalities as Poulenc and Satie.

Still stranger by contrast to Lancastrian relations and protégées, who, together with a few school friends, had hitherto made up my social world, was the Roquebrune circle in which the Van dens moved, for almost all were concerned with the arts, and business and politics were never mentioned. Even when, as occasionally happened, a Belgian friend arrived on a visit, whom one learnt was in fact 'un grand industriel' or 'le premier chirurgien de Bruxelles', he was as likely as not immediately to seat himself at the piano and play half a dozen Bach fugues at a stretch. Among the close friends and neighbours were Simon Bussy, Gabriel Hanoteaux, and Paul Valéry. Names such as Matisse and Stravinsky, which had hitherto sounded in my ears as remote as Ingres or Beethoven, occurred constantly in the conversation as those of friends and acquaintances, while the post regularly brought long letters and sheaves of magnificent photographs from M. Gide at that time voyaging in the Congo. Nor could the width of the gulf separating this circle from that of my family be wholly attributed to differences of nationality for at least two English figures, Roger Fry and Dorothy Bussy, were regular members. But Gordon Square and Putney Hill, I soon realised, were far, far more than a sixpenny bus-ride apart.

Most adolescents are, I suppose, at some time or other, filled with a snobbish shame at the supposed inadequacy, social, intellectual or political, of their families. The reaction this induces changes according to the climate of the period; in my own case it led to an uncritical rejection of all the artistic values which my parents still upheld, and a ridiculous exaltation of contemporary masters at the expense of those they revered, which found expression in the illogical view that because Proust was a great novelist, Dickens could not be; five years later it would have taken the form of joining the Communist party and maintaining that no essential difference divided Fascists and Tories.

Having quickly adapted myself to what I imagined to be the intellectual outlook of 'La Couala' I was tortured with anxiety as to how unspeakably bourgeois and philistine must the Van dens have found the Lancasters during their sojourn in England.

What could they have thought, I asked myself, of the bogus Dutch landscapes, the Academy portraits, the heraldic furniture of South Lynn? How bored and horrified must they have been in a household where a total unawareness of the world of ideas not only existed but was regarded as a matter for congratulation, and where all the arts, save one, were judged to be but enjoyable pastimes,

69

more praiseworthy than bridge but less ennobling than riding. In particular the Lancastrian attitude to the only art which they did consider perhaps more easily justified (largely on moral grounds) than the rest—music—must, I felt, have been peculiarly unsympathetic.

In this last supposition, it must be admitted, I had some justification, for the theory that music was 'a good thing' produced in practice some very strange results. My grandfather's failure completely to master the violin late in life, a failure which the more critical of his long-suffering relations considered he was an unconscionable time in accepting, had determined him that none of his family should have to go through life similarly ill-equipped. Thus my Aunt Mary, who almost alone of the family had some genuine musical feeling, was an extremely competent clarinettist; my Uncle Harry's rich and confident baritone had easily gained him a place in the Bach choir and combined with a handsome presence earned him many a request to 'bring his music' when dining out; and my Aunt Hetty, although never a carefree, was nevertheless an infinitely painstaking performer of Beethoven's easier piano pieces. As the third generation advanced in years various gaps in the ensemble were steadily filled. My cousin Barbara, who had inherited something of her mother's skill, was allotted the 'cello; my Cousin Peggy took over her grandfather's violin, a choice which only he, rendered indulgent perhaps by his personal experience of the difficulties of the instrument and protected, moreover, by almost total deafness, regarded as anything but unfortunate; her sister Ruth had come to be considered as having a very pretty contralto, although few went so far as to maintain an equally satisfactory ear; and to me fell that beautiful, but temperamental instrument, the flute.

On ceremonial occasions, such as my grandfather's birthday or Christmas, we all arrived carrying our instruments and each equipped with some little concert piece laboriously practised for many months beforehand. The great object of the whole exercise, that all my grandfather's descendants should combine in some single paean of praise or thanksgiving, was never, alas, achieved, partly due to the fact that few composers seem to have worked for just this exact combination of instruments and voices, and partly to the rather varied degrees of accomplishment to which the performers had attained. This was doubly unfortunate for not only did it prolong the agony but also gave rise to internecine feuds and rivalries. While all had to admit little Barbara's remarkable

mastery of the 'cello, some thought it was rather an ungainly instrument for a girl, and although few, except her own parents, pretended to have much pleasure from little Ruth's rendering of 'Tit-willow', more, perhaps, might have made the effort. My own show-piece 'La Paloma' was usually greeted with a due appreciation of its difficulty, but some there were who appeared by their reception of it to assume a non-existent comic intent on the part of the composer.

Painful as these occasions had been at the time, they had become doubly so in recollection. It was, therefore, with considerable satisfaction that I reflected, while listening to Miss Van den giving a masterly rendering of Poulenc's 'La Bestiaire', that to such musical evenings as her parents may have had to endure at South Lynn I had been debarred by my age from contributing personally.

As the picture which the Van dens retained of life at South Lynn was gradually unfolded in conversation and reminiscence it provided, in its patent unlikeness to the sombre and embarrassing conception which my nervous imagination had built up, a chastening and much-needed lesson. It was true that they had not been much impressed by either the musical understanding nor the executive ability revealed in the family concerts, but the grand-paternal enthusiasm which had prompted them they considered wholly praiseworthy. My grandfather himself they regarded as the beau ideal of 'le grand seigneur anglais' and in the highest degree aristocratic. Here, I think they were misled by that rather too exclusively chivalric conception of the honour of knighthood still current abroad, for while my grandfather could rightly be described as patriarchal, possibly even patrician, aristocratic was, strictly speaking, an overstatement. Far more astonishing, however, was the tribute they paid to his intellect. His complete lack of sympathy with the sort of art they practised and admired in no way surprised them but his tolerance and freedom from all affectation in such matters they thought unusual and wholly admirable. His literary judgements which were confined to English and the classics, they were prepared to accept unquestioningly, and they had been deeply impressed by his privately printed volume of verse, of the very existence of which I was now made for the first time somewhat apprehensively aware. For his way of life, for the whole complicated machine of South Lynn existence, with its unalterable mealtimes, its Sabbath calm, its starched maid-servants, its gleaming carriages, they expressed the most genuine admiration. And if this admiration had something in common with the fascinated delight of the anthropologist over some perfectly preserved example of a culture hitherto thought to be extinct, it was based on a full appreciation of the moral values that lay beneath.

Only once had the Van dens' understanding failed them, and this on the only occasion on which my grandfather had displayed that Jove-like side to his character of which his family were always so nervously aware. In some discussion of English literature M. Van den had chanced to speak appreciatively of Oscar Wilde and the reaction had proved the more alarming for being wholly unexpected. His host's expression had immediately become thunderous and in a tone of awful gravity ('c'etait une voix terrible, vous savez') he had been informed that had he not been a foreigner he would have realised that that was a name which could never be mentioned in a gentleman's house. While this confusion of moral and aesthetic judgements had remained for ever inexplicable the incident itself had undoubtedly left a deep impression, for I noticed that while during my stay with the Van dens the works not only of Stendhal and Fromentin, but of such contemporary writers as Valéry and Claudel, were pressed on me, my fondness for Proust met with little encouragement and the only work of their friend M. Gide which I was led to study was *Isabelle*.

The doubts of the validity of my personal conception of my grandfather's character which the Van dens' recollections had sown were strengthened soon after my return to England. My grandfather who was by this time a very old man had recently taken to his bed for almost the first time in his life and there was a certain urgency about the summons to South Lynn which awaited me. On arrival I was taken straight up to his bedroom, an apartment I now penetrated for the first time, overlooking the tops of the elm-trees in The Field and the wooded heights of East Putney deceptively rural-looking in the late afternoon sun. He was sitting up in bed, rather thinner than I remembered him, his white beard flowing over woollen pyjamas and with his hands, palm down, lying flat on the coverlet. His eyes had a slightly glazed look and there was a heavy charnel house smell in the room, but his voice was as firm as ever. As we talked, in a studiously matter-of-fact way, it suddenly occurred to me for the first time, that despite the impression created by his unshakable joviality, my grandfather was not, and had not been for a long time, a happy man: and that

73

as he now looked back on his life he did not feel quite the satisfaction which he might justifiably have expected.

On the face of it, it was hard to see what had gone wrong, for if ever a man had fully accomplished what he set out to do that man was my grandfather. An only son of a widowed mother, largely dependent on the charity of friends for his education, he had, in his 'teens, set forth on the stage coach from Lynn to Cambridge which was as far as the railway at that time reached, determined to make his way in London and restore his family to their former affluence. In this he had completely succeeded, making a fortune large enough for him to discharge all his obligations many times over. Anyone claiming the remotest connection with the family, or whose parents or grandparents had had any hand in his education, was liberally rewarded. He had completely rebuilt and re-equipped the grammar school which had given him an education for which he had always been deeply grateful; he had founded prizes and scholarships and endowed hospital beds and charities without number; he had restored churches (not always, admittedly, with the happiest results) and erected innumerable memorials. His marriage had been singularly happy, and his pride in his children was manifest if uncritical. Why, then, should I have gained so distinct an impression that as he surveyed his life from his death-bed he found something lacking: that while his career testified so strikingly to the truth of the assumption that if a man wants anything sufficiently strongly he will always get it, it yet quite failed to contradict the rider that this is only too likely to happen after he had ceased to want it?

His life, it was true, had not been wholly free from disappointments and sorrows; his electoral campaigns had never been crowned with success, and several of the beneficiaries of his educational enthusiasm had turned out unsatisfactorily, notably one highly promising lad who had won every conceivable scholarship and exhibition only to go, immediately on leaving the University, straight to Hollywood. These, however, were minor blows. Infinitely graver were the death of his wife, after a few years of blissfully happy marriage, and the fact that two of his sons, and

74

those perhaps the best loved, had predeceased him. Nevertheless, the abiding sorrow which these losses had brought seemed in so resilient a character the effect rather than the cause of a deeper melancholy, and one, moreover, which could certainly not be attributed to universal causes, for his religious faith, though simple, was robust, and never, I think, for a moment was he visited by any doubts as to the justice of an economic system which he so perfectly understood and which had brought him such prosperity.

On looking back it seems to me that the trouble may have lain in the very perfection of his achievement; that while his success story had followed so undeviatingly the classic lines he himself was, fundamentally, a romantic, and a frustrated one at that. In support of this view I can only call up small scraps of unrelated evidence, by themselves of no great significance, perhaps, but which when combined provide, if not proof, at least an indication. That strangely feminine mouth which according to the boyhood portrait lurked beneath the beard; the desperate violin playing and the privately printed poems; even the slightly ridiculous passion for heraldry which certainly had in it nothing of the snobbish. And in addition a scrap of conversation which has stuck in my mind through the years.

One night after dinner he told me, apropos of some genealogical discussion, that at a time when he was in constant correspondence with the College of Heralds, he had received a letter from an old antiquary in Norwich upbraiding him for relinquishing the crest which the family had up till that time borne in favour of a new grant of arms, adding the information that the former dated from a time long past when the Lancasters had been the largest landowners in the county. "Complete nonsense, of course," said my grandfather, "and not worth the expense and trouble of following up." But the tone of voice in which this forthright piece of common sense was pronounced indicated quite clearly that in his heart of hearts he held the exactly contrary view.

In fact the head had here attained too complete a victory over the heart, a fact which my grandfather, I suspect, had himself come half to realise, though never to admit. For it was impossible

75

to think of him ever undertaking any action, of making any gesture, without due consideration, and while naturally the most kind-hearted of men, he had long ago convinced himself, perfectly rightly, that even kindness, if it is to attain its maximum effect, must be directed and thought out.

Thus, while I have no doubt that the hints of the Norwich antiquary brought instantly before his inner eye an impossibly glamorous world peopled with mythical Lancasters in shining armour ablaze with heraldry, a glittering mediaeval never-never-land in the probably quite fruitless exploration of which he would have had infinite pleasure, I am equally certain that a still small voice had pointed out to him that while a certain degree of interest in one's forebears and their quarterings was perfectly appropriate to the hero of a Victorian success story, to pursue it too far would not only involve unjustifiable time and expense but lay one open to ridicule and sarcasm.

It may well be that these reflections were in fact quite baseless; that I was only driven thus to speculate by the feeling that this was, or should have been, a dramatic moment; and the very fact that there was no heightening of the tension led me to give an unwarranted significance to its absence. But whether or not the emotion was purely subjective, I was, at that moment, for the first time made suddenly and vividly aware of one of the central facts of human existence—the terrifying isolation of the individual and the resultant impossibility of ever really knowing another human being. For I felt that if ever I were to receive an answer to the riddle which had for so long puzzled me, of what exactly my grand-father was like beneath the protecting envelope of bearded *bon-homie*, it should have been now, and no answer was forthcoming.

Certainly nothing in this final interview lent any support to my thwarted romantic theory. Our conversation was factual in the extreme, ranging over my progress at Oxford, the desirability of my being called to the Bar, and what London Clubs it would be suitable for me to join, and was brought to an end by a firm hand-shake and a "Well, good-bye, my boy, I don't suppose I shall be seeing you again". Feeling more than usually inadequate I turned to go and had already reached the door when I was called back. Handing me a sheet of paper and a stamped envelope my grandfather asked me if I would mind giving the former to my Aunt Kate and put the latter out for posting. Examining them on the way downstairs I noticed that on the paper was a list of numbers relating to Hymns A. and M. ending with the 'Dead March in Saul', and the envelope was addressed in a firm clear hand,

> The Editor,
> (Obituaries)
> *The Times*,
> Printing House Square.

4. "There was I waiting at the church"

THERE IS no silence in the world so overwhelming as
that which prevails on a small country station when a train
has just left. The fact that it is by no means complete, that
the fading echoes of the engine are still clearly audible from beyond
the signal-box behind which the guard's van is finally disappearing, that one now hears for the first time the cawing of the rooks,
a distant dog's bark, the hum of the bees in the station-master's
garden, in no way detracts from its quality. The rattling world of
points and sleepers, of gossiping fellow-passengers and sepia views
of Cromer beach has been whirled away leaving a void which, for
some moments yet, the sounds and smells of the countryside will
be powerless to fill.

At Eastwinch station, lost amidst the un-by-passed fields of my
Edwardian childhood, this period of suspension was apt to be
longer than elsewhere. The platform, though I suppose no higher
than most, appeared in the flat East Anglian landscape to be a
raised island, isolated way above the surrounding elm-broken

cornlands. Nor did it ever, at first glance, exhibit any sign of life, as the solitary porter's immediate duty was to open the level-crossing gates regardless of the passengers, alone with their luggage amidst the shiny tinplates advertising Stephens' Blueblack Ink and Venos Lightning Cough Cure. And it was only just as we were beginning to wonder whether or not this was the right day, that an aunt would suddenly emerge from the waiting-room.

Her greeting never varied. After the usual brisk, no-nonsense kiss and the routine enquiries she would announce that Jones had brought the trap (the Renault was never sent to the station save for my grandfather himself or some guest of more than usual age or decrepitude) and would take Nurse and the luggage, but that she expected that Osbert would like a little walk after all that time in the stuffy train. This was always said with a richly sardonic smile, she knowing full well that there was nothing Osbert so much abominated as little walks, no matter how many hours had been spent in stuffy trains; he, however, had long since learnt the use-lessness of protest and would inevitably find himself a few minutes later trudging along the Station Road gazing regretfully at Nurse, comfortably ensconced in the trap, bowling briskly away in a cloud of dust.

Even today Eastwinch is a very small village; at that date it was smaller still. Small, that is, judged by the number of its inhabitants rather than by its extent. Strung out for a mile or more along the Lynn-Swaffham road it started at the Lynn end with the church, a decent enough fourteenth-century Norfolk structure without, but scraped and scrubbed into insignificance within by the late Sir Gilbert Scott, standing on an outlying ridge of the Breckland, that scruffy, sandy waste which runs like some horrid birthmark across the homely face of East Anglia. Alongside, dank and laurel-shaded, was the vicarage; beyond, down the hill, lay the straight village street, hardly differing in character from the rest of the highway, so widely separated were the cottages, the four public-houses (two of them no longer licensed since my grandfather had decided that the needs of the villagers were being, perhaps, too amply cared for), and the solitary village shop. Half a mile beyond the point where it was entered by the Station Road, an ordinary country lane crossing the branch line from Lynn some three-quarters of a mile away, the street ended in a sharp fork, in the apex of which, facing directly up the village to the church, stood the imposing, globe-topped entrance gates of Eastwinch Hall.

The gates, once entered, were generally felt to be an overstatement. On the right lay a croquet lawn screened from the converg-

ing roads by a plantation of copper beeches; less than a hundred yards ahead was the house itself. Built a century earlier by some modest nabob who had done well in the tea trade, tradition maintained that it had been deliberately designed on the model of a tea-caddy. Although at the time I never dreamed of doubting this theory, on looking back it seems to me to have been a perfectly ordinary, four-square late Georgian residence with a rather low-pitched roof. Such idiosyncrasies as it displayed were all, in fact, the work of my grandfather; they took the form of terra-cotta masks of Comedy and Tragedy with which he had seen fit to enliven the plain expanse of yellow brick between the first and second storeys, unexpected bow-windows bulging out on ground level, and a vast gabled porch masking the front door. The erection of this last had unfortunately coincided with the height of the old gentleman's genealogical enthusiasm, and the pediment was adorned with a highly baroque version of his coat of arms in terra-cotta. So unexpectedly heavy had this forthright statement of the Lancaster family's inclusion among the armigerous classes proved that the fretted and white-painted wooden supports were already visibly straining beneath their burden of heraldry.

Structurally unsound and decoratively over-emphatic, the front porch nevertheless provided the focal point round which, during the long summer days, the whole life of the house revolved. Here my grandfather would sit reading his day-old *Times*, and to it would come the gardener with his offering of flowers which my aunts would painstakingly 'arrange' in a series of unattractive vases lined up on the tiled floor. As a vantage point from which nurses and parents could keep an eye on the younger children, and sporting uncles could give unsolicited advice to tennis-playing nephews and nieces, it was in constant demand. And always, on arrival, one found there the whole house-party grouped in a welcoming tableau.

I here use the word house-party simply as a convenient noun of assembly, disregarding its overtones. For us, particularly when speaking of the years before the first German war, the term has taken on a certain glamour, suggesting almost exclusively assemblies of the smart and the beautiful pursuing worldly pleasures in a constantly changed variety of expensive clothes. Nothing could bear less resemblance to the gatherings at Eastwinch Hall; no baccarat scandals ever darkened the fair name of a house where the only permitted card games were strictly educational; the conversation was seldom of a brilliance to have fired the imagination of Mr. Henry James; and it can safely be said that never, never did these corridors echo to whispered speculations about the geography of the bedrooms.

The two over-riding interests of my grandfather's life were his family and philanthropy. The first made it difficult for him, although fundamentally a social character, to take any great pleasure in the company under his own roof of those who were not in some way connected with the clan; the second provided ample opportunities for the employment of his large fortune without having recourse to the pursuit of expensive social ambitions. However, as the only son of an only son, despite the fact that of his seven children all but two had married and produced families, his circle would have been more restricted than he liked had not his genealogical researches helped to extend it. Diligent combing of the further branches of the family tree had revealed the existence of extraordinary survivals from a long-vanished Norfolk of gloomy farmers and manic-depressive yeomen. Unfortunately these had turned out to be exclusively female, and while they afforded many opportunities for the exercise of philanthropy their social gifts were seldom of an order effectively to enrich life at the Hall. They had, therefore, been comfortably installed in small villas on the outskirts of Lynn and in cosy cottages dotted round the country where their maintenance had been made the responsibility of my father and uncles. Deeply and volubly appreciative of their good fortune they were known collectively as the Grateful Hearts but seldom asked to the house.

In course of time the place which they should have taken had been filled by a second outer circle of Grateful Hearts differing in certain important respects from the original collection. Although its members could boast no blood relationship with the family they had all, at some time or another, been connected with it, usually in a dependent capacity. For inclusion in this group from which house-guests were selected three things, beyond a modicum of gentility, were necessary—poverty, piety and physical affliction. Naturally the senior members had soon developed so highly skilled a technique for the display of these attributes that a certain rivalry had sprung up. In my day the two prized exhibits, between whose merits no distinction was possible, were Miss Childs and Miss Marple. The former was an elderly lady of extreme bad temper suffering from advanced cataract; the latter a kindly, timid creature with curvature of the spine. While Miss Childs could rightly claim cataract as the worse affliction, Miss Marple was undoubtedly the poorer, and as their piety was equal and unquestioned there could be no supremacy on points. The fact that Miss Marple in addition to her hump-back had also a heavy cavalry moustache did not count, as the Lancasters themselves were a hirsute lot (one of my great-aunts had several times been mistaken for Lord Kitchener), and among them such an adornment was considered rather a source of pride than of shame.

The runners-up in these depressing stakes were undoubtedly Mr. and Mrs. Phipps. The husband, a seedy clergyman who was still, at an advanced age, a curate in the West of England, was generally known among the younger generation as 'Filthy Phipps' from the fact that his neck and hands invariably matched the greasy black of his clerical boater. His wife, a faded and depressed woman only slightly cleaner than her husband, suffered from an obscure malady the exact nature of which remained undisclosed. To this and to Mr. Phipps' guaranteed professional piety they owed their position, but remained debarred from further advancement by a certain whining dissatisfaction with their lot. For it was *de rigueur* that all afflictions should be bravely and brightly borne.

Rather less secure was the position of Frau Schmiegelow. Originally my aunts' German governess, this stout Prussian was bidden from time to time to quit her native land and revisit her former pupils. Her piety, which was of the aggressively Lutheran kind, was undoubted, and thanks to an unfortunate marriage to the postmaster of a small town in Schleswig-Holstein, her poverty was assured. At her afflictions it was more difficult, at first sight, to guess; extremely well-covered and bursting with health and self-assurance it was far from easy to see how she qualified on this score. It was rumoured that the postmaster drank, but what was an alcoholic husband compared to cataract or curvature of the spine? Looking back I now realise that her affliction was held to lie in her foreign birth. Not to be English was for my family so terrible a handicap as almost to place the sufferer in the permanent invalid class: the only difference being that, while it was the height of uncharitableness to laugh at invalids, foreigners were always legitimate targets for a robust sense of fun.

In the case of Frau Schmiegelow this grave disadvantage was, of course, mitigated by the fact that she was a German, for if one had to be foreign it was far better to be German, preferably a Prussian. Not only did the Lancasters find in the Germans all those virtues which they most admired—discipline, industry, physical courage and simple, unaffected Evangelical piety—but several of them had completed their education in Germany and all spoke the language fluently. Indeed, had the Germans only possessed a sense of humour they might almost have qualified as honorary Englishmen. In Frau Schmiegelow's case this deficiency was principally apparent in her attitude to Wilhelm II, a personality whom her hosts regarded as richly comic; and while good manners prevented this source of quiet fun from being exploited too openly, the gluey, hypnotised reverence with which the devoted Frau pronounced the syllables "der liebe Kaiser" strained forbearance to the utmost.

However, although occasionally a trial, Frau Schmiegelow nevertheless served a useful social purpose in consolidating the opinion of the other Grateful Hearts and, by her provocative advocacy of her sovereign's merits, in restoring a unity which at times showed signs of strain. In Frau Schmiegelow's presence Miss Childs, who was very Low, would forget for a moment her annoyance at the ecclesiastical lace on which Miss Marple, who was very High, was for ever engaged. (Despite her affliction some sixth sense enabled Miss Childs to be instantly aware of the Paschal Lamb or Sacred Monogram taking shape beneath the clever fingers of her rival.) Similarly Miss Marple, confronted with the greater menace, would overlook the fact of the Reverend Phipps' notorious indifference to the Eastward Position; while the Phipps themselves ceased for a few moments to be consumed by the jealousy constantly provoked by the greater regard in which the two old spinsters were generally held.

So powerfully, indeed, did the other Grateful Hearts react to

Frau Schmiegelow that she was able to exercise her restorative spell even by remote control. In the summers immediately preceding 1914, when her visits had ceased, the mere sight of her thin Gothic writing on an envelope was sufficient to promote harmony, while her lyrical account of the All-Highest's latest speech at Kiel or Potsdam, which one of my aunts would always make a point of immediately translating, produced a gratifying unanimity lasting for several days.

Far more powerful than poor Frau Schmiegelow's was the personality, and infinitely more disruptive the influence, of Miss Redpath. Whereas the other Grateful Hearts live on in my memory distinct but flat, Miss Redpath remains a three-dimensional figure, fully realised and complete. Indeed she was the first person outside my immediate family of whose individuality I was fully aware, and even as a very small child I was always conscious that she was not to be ranged with the lay-figures on the porch, whom I could not conceive of as functioning away from their familiar base, but enjoyed an independent existence far beyond the confines of the Hall. Nor was this difference merely apparent; Miss Redpath in fact fulfilled none of the conditions attached to the status of a Grateful Heart. Although by no means rich she had a small income of her own; her good health, despite the fact that she was well over seventy, was aggressive; and so far from being pious, or even indifferent to religion, she was a convinced and militant agnostic.

Lacking all the necessary stigmata it was difficult at first to explain her inclusion among us. If, as it is charitable to suppose, her hostesses were prompted by a disinterested desire to help and give pleasure to the lonely and unfortunate, it was quite obvious that she rightly considered herself in no way distressed, nor did she conceal the fact that she had a host of friends and that Eastwinch was only one of several country houses that she would be visiting in the course of the summer. If, as was sometimes disloyally suggested by their in-laws, the Lancasters suffered from an ingrained distaste for the company of their equals and were only really happy when surrounded by those they were in a position to patronise, then one would have said it would have been impossible to find a more difficult subject for the exercise of this discreditable family weakness than Miss Redpath.

The real reason, I fancy, why every summer this forthright and unaccommodating figure appeared for a week or a fortnight was, largely, fear. She had been the extremely capable Principal of the excellent girls' school at which my mother and my aunts (and indeed even some of my great-aunts) had received their education, and the awe in which they still held her made it impossible for them, having once asked her, to discontinue their invitations. Moreover she was a firm favourite of my grandfather who sometimes, I think, was hard put to it to conceal the boredom which the company of his other guests induced, and who fully appreciated the masculine qualities of her extremely well-trained mind.

Miss Redpath's appearance was completely in keeping with her character. Although very small, the extreme rigidity of her bearing fully compensated for any lack of inches, and her square face, with its great width of jaw, was distinguished by two peculiarities of expression which greatly added to the awe which she inspired. Her eyes always kept a look of astonished ferocity due to the fact that the bright blue irises were surrounded by a complete circle of white, their circumference nowhere broken by the lids, a phenomenon I have only otherwise observed among professional hypnotists and in photographs of Mussolini. In speaking she was never known to move her jaw, so that behind her exaggeratedly mobile lips (she was always very particular about elocution and would never tolerate 'mumbling') one was always conscious of the rigidly clenched teeth. Her costume, which was well chosen to set off her personality, never varied. Her coat and skirt of rich purple broadcloth trimmed with black braid were cut to allow the maximum movement; her black boots were thick and sensible; and beneath the high lace collar supported on either side by little serpentine wires one could clearly distinguish the vigorous movement of the neck-muscles occasioned by her peculiar manner of speech.

Whereas my cousins and the majority of their parents regarded the coming of Miss Redpath with marked apprehension I looked forward to it with the keenest pleasure. Not only had I long since discounted her alarming appearance and abrupt manner (for I had frequently been taken by my mother to visit her in London) but I much appreciated her powers as a story-teller and the fact that in addressing children she did not consider it necessary to adopt a manner of speaking in any way different from that in which she conversed with their elders. Moreover she lived in what I firmly considered to be the most beautiful house in the world.

In my childhood the sight of the trim green lawns of Hampstead Garden Suburb shaded by the carefully preserved elms, the white-painted posts linked by chains, the leaded casements and tile-hung gables, above all the miniature scale on which everything was conceived, induced a feeling of inexpressible delight; a feeling that suffered no lessening when the green-painted front door of Miss R.'s residence, with its heartshaped, bottle-glazed wicket, was finally opened.

Miss Redpath was a cousin of one of the leading Pre-Raphael-ites (I think Holman Hunt) and the interior of her house had already acquired a strong period flavour. Immediately on entering one was confronted with a large reproduction of 'May Morning on Magdalen Tower' with an affectionate message from the artist scrawled on the mount, and on all sides one was conscious of Burne-Jones maidens yearning at one in sanguine chalk above bosky thickets of honesty and cape-gooseberries tastefully arranged in polished copper pots. Elsewhere were many brass-rubbings of recumbent knights and innumerable Arundel prints, while the presence of several Della Robbia plaques, a set of faded, purplish photographs of the Gozzoli frescoes in the Medici Chapel and some small, painstaking water-colours of Assisi, indicated that their owner shared to the full the Italophil enthusiasm of the late Victorians. The two small ground-floor rooms in which, against Morris wallpapers, all these treasures were displayed were connected by an open arch so that it was possible on the moment of entry to see right through the house to the little orchard beyond.

This, besides filling the interior with a green, filtered light, invariably suggested to me the scene that would be revealed were one to walk through the range of buildings in the background of Millais' *Autumn Leaves*.

Whether or not my childish whimseys were far-fetched, it was certain that no apartments could be further removed in atmosphere from the interior of Eastwinch Hall, but so powerful was the impression they created that Miss Redpath, who was not in herself a romantic figure, when seen against the familiar background of pitch-pine panelling, foxed sporting prints, and stuffed birds allegedly shot by an uncle in the Fayyum, still trailed clouds of Italo-Arthurian glory.

Nevertheless, there was nothing of the 'greenery-yallery' about her; a daughter of the manse she had learnt Latin and Greek at her father's knee, had been among the very first women to graduate at Bedford College, and was a distinguished Anglo-Saxon scholar, the friend and pupil of Professor Skeat. In addition she was a foundation member of the Fabian Society and a convinced, if not militant, Suffragette. Her standards of judgement were, therefore, high, and while her admiration for the achievements of the Pre-Raphaelites and their contemporaries was sincere it by no means invariably extended to their personalities.

It will readily be understood that the annual appearance of Miss Redpath, then at the height of her powers, in the close and docile circle of the Hall, was attended by a certain heightening of tension. Both sides, it is true, made allowances; my aunts for their part, although never finally abandoning hope of their old mistress's ultimate conversion, forewent the pleasure of open proselytising, while she made a genuine, if sometimes rather too obvious, effort to suffer fools gladly and to achieve the soft answer which turneth away wrath. Nevertheless, all present were conscious of the strain which steadily increased as her visit drew to its appointed close and it was obvious that sooner or later someone would go too far. I count it among the great privileges of my childhood that when the inevitable happened I was an eye-witness.

The day of Miss Redpath's downfall was a Sunday; a fact which, besides providing the very circumstances of the disaster, immeasurably heightened the drama. For at Eastwinch Hall even so late as the early years of George V the Victorian Sabbath retained all its rigours unmodified. Whatever books we had been reading during the week were put away and their places taken by bound volumes of *The Quiver*, dating from the period of my father's childhood. For me personally this was no great hardship as it merely involved handing in the G. A. Henty which had been my ostensible reading for the week while retaining concealed the W. W. Jacobs which I had been devouring under cover. Besides I rather enjoyed *The Quiver*; I was developing a keen period sense and derived much simple pleasure from the wood-engravings of whiskered curates and bonneted social workers. But my poor cousins, whose home-life was more emancipated than mine, were less resigned; already condemned, owing to our remoteness from any centre of modern civilisation, to miss at least three vital sequences of the *Perils of Pauline*, they regarded the weekly confiscation of *Comic Cuts* and *Buffalo Bill* as the most unjustifiable and high-handed curtailment of personal liberty. And their lot was rendered all the harder by the strict rules governing Sunday games, which I for my part rather welcomed. For after a week of humiliating and unrelieved defeat on the tennis court the enforced substitution of croquet, at which I early manifested a careless mastery, caused me no pain. But even the right to play croquet had been a hardly won concession granted only on appeal to my grandfather. He had ruled, very sensibly, that whereas the tennis-court was visible from the road and the vicar feared that the spectacle of the gentry at play might lead the villagers into sin, the croquet-lawn was concealed by a dense shrubbery so that only our own salvation was imperilled, and this was a risk which he thought, on the whole, we were justified in taking. Clock-golf, however, remained a bone of contention, my cousins maintaining that it was only a form of croquet and equally well-concealed, my aunts sticking firmly to the belief that it was in some way a 'worldlier' sport and therefore unsuited to the Lord's Day.

This particular Sunday dawned bright and fair with a brisk

wind sending small white clouds scudding across the vast East Anglian sky. As it was not the first Sunday in the month only Miss Marple had gone to Early Service, and the house party, with the exception of Miss Redpath, assembled for the first time at family prayers. When these were at long last concluded and the domestic staff in their unfamiliar morning prints had bustled back to their own quarters, all trooped in to breakfast where, as usual, the conversation turned exclusively on the events of the previous twelve hours.

One of the principal differences between our parents' generation and our own would seem to be that their nights were so much more tightly packed with incident. Not only were they constantly assailed by the pangs of hunger in the small hours, so that even in so austere a house as the Hall a tin of Marie biscuits stood at every visitor's bedside, but they never, apparently, enjoyed a single night of unbroken slumber. On this occasion Miss Childs had been aroused by the most extraordinary noise around midnight, while Miss Marple had been so convinced that there was a bat in her room that she had not dared to light her candle. And whatever door was it that had banged so persistently? My aunt said that she had been so certain that it was the upstairs bathroom that she had actually gone to close it only to find it firmly shut. And would somebody please remind her to speak to Scarlett about cutting back the Virginia creeper over the front porch as, really, last night the noise it made scraping against the landing window was too uncanny? As usual the conversation was only brought to an end by one of the ladies appealing to my father for confirmation of some particular nocturnal phenomenon and receiving the reply that he had heard nothing as, unlike some people, he went to bed to sleep.

Breakfast over I was summoned by my grandfather to take part in the elaborate Sunday morning ritual at which all the grandchildren took it in turns to assist. First I went into the hall and fetched the freshly cut rose left by the gardener in a particular little vase on the hall-table, and returning to the breakfast-room slipped it neatly into my grandfather's button-hole. Then I waited, matches ready, while he carefully selected a handful of cigars for his case, reserving one for immediate smoking which he finally placed in his mouth very slowly, as if even he were not quite sure of the exact whereabouts of that feature, lost amidst the hawthorn hedgerows of his beard. After we were both satisfied that it was truly alight and drawing properly, I departed to the gun-room and removed with almost sacramental care from the locker, where it was kept neatly folded throughout the week, a Union Jack. Taking this carefully under my arm I rejoined my grandfather on the porch and we both then marched at a solemn pace across the tennis lawn to where, close by the road, there rose a flagpole.

Looking back I confess myself slightly puzzled by my family's passion for flagpoles; no member of it, except a half-legendary great-uncle, said to have served as a cabin-boy on the *Bellerophon*, had ever been in the Navy, nor had any of them lived in those far-flung outposts of Empire where showing the flag is an established ritual. Nevertheless, all of them in their country houses, and frequently in London as well if the garden was sufficiently large to allow of them doing so without inviting ridicule, had erected these impressive totems. However, in those pre-Freudian days the field of speculation was limited and I had long since come to accept a flagpole as being as normal an adjunct to a gentleman's residence as a greenhouse or a bathroom.

Once the bunting was safely aloft my mind was immediately occupied with a single overriding care—to avoid, in the short time that remained before Church, being sent to the lavatory. This anxiety had no physiological nor psychological foundation but arose quite naturally from the local plumbing arrangements. The single water-closet at the Hall was strictly reserved for the use of females; all the masculine members of the party, provided they were in good health, were expected to go to the earth closet which was housed in a tasteful neo-classic building discreetly surrounded by laurels, adjoining the stables. Unfortunately this structure was of wood and in the course of time a plank had worked loose at the back allowing the chickens, which were constantly straying into the stable-yard, free access at ground level. Originally this had intrigued rather than worried me, but ever since I had received a sharp nip on the tenderest, and at the time the most exposed, portion of my anatomy, my daily visits had been rendered hideous by fear and apprehension. With the usual false shame of childhood I had never revealed the cause of my reluctance, which was put down to obstinacy or constipation or both and treated accordingly. On week-days there was no possibility of escape, but just occasionally on Sundays my nurse and parents would be too busy getting ready for Divine Service to remember to make the usual enquiries.

Whether or not on this occasion I succeeded in avoiding my fate I cannot now recall, but I was certainly present, brushed and tidy, a quarter of an hour later, when the house party was assembled ready on the porch, the ladies all elaborately gloved and veiled and the gentlemen in dark suits and Homburg hats, for the frock coats and silk hats which were still *de rigueur* for urban worship had come by this date to be considered a little too ostentatious in the country. The only non-starter was Miss Redpath whose absence was perfectly well understood and resolutely ignored.

Ignored, that is, by the grown-ups but not by my Cousin John, a relentlessly inquisitive youth with an insatiable desire for information.

"Auntie, where's Miss Redpath?"

"That's nothing to do with you, dear."

"Auntie, isn't Miss Redpath coming to Church?"

Silence.

"Auntie, why isn't Miss Redpath coming to Church?"

Even then I well understood the nature of the dilemma with which my unfortunate relatives were thus confronted, for when it came to a strict regard for truth Matilda's aunt had nothing on mine. Their whole life was based on abhorrence of the Lie, and their definition of what constituted an untruth was wide indeed. All prevarication, euphemism and tactful understatement were for them impossible and resolutely to be discouraged in others. Often I myself, always an imaginative child, had been pulled up short in some harmless exaggeration by the soft question "Osbert dear, is that quite true?" In my younger days I found these exalted standards slightly ridiculous but now, when the politicians and the advertisers and the propagandists have succeeded in hiding the face of truth behind a thick veil of sophistry and illusion, the uncompromising attitude of my aunts (which I am happy to say they both maintain completely unabated at this present day) appears to me in a wholly admirable, if uncomfortably brilliant, light.

Truth, however, is notoriously a two-edged sword and on this occasion its revelation was attended with the gravest perils. To give the real reason for Miss Redpath's non-appearance would not only destroy our childish faith in the undeviating orthodoxy of all grown-up persons, and with it our respect, but it would reveal to us for the first time, and in the most unfortunate way, the existence of Doubt. For ordinary mortals it would have been possible to say that Miss Redpath had a headache—but not for my aunts; which was, perhaps, just as well because at that very moment the subject of the discussion was clearly visible marching off down the drive for one of her six-mile walks. Their normal reaction would then have been to have said that John must ask her himself, but they well knew that their nephew was a literal-minded and persistent lad who would undoubtedly act on this suggestion at the first opportunity, when Miss Redpath would unhesitatingly give her reasons accurately and at length. Finally after unavailing efforts to ignore the whole business they went so far as to say that Miss Redpath did not wish to come *this time*, hoping thus to give the impression that her absence was something quite uncustomary, and briskly started up a general conversation on other topics in which the Grateful Hearts loyally and loudly joined.

The interior of Eastwinch Church although of noble proportions was utterly without character. So well had Sir Gilbert done his work that, even for so romantic a mediaevalist as I then was, the scraped pillars and recut capitals had no message. All I can now remember is the extreme brightness and newness of the fittings. The crimson of the fleur-de-lys patterned felt which carpeted the chancel and covered the hassocks was hardly less startling than that of Elijah's robe in the East window; the brass oil-lamps rising above the stripped pine pews shone with a celestial brightness; and so dazzling was the lectern that it almost hurt to look at it.

The service itself, it must be confessed, displayed rather less sparkle, and was only enlivened for me by the recurrent astonishment I always experienced on hearing grown-ups sing. It was not so much the actual fact of their singing which amazed, but the feeling they put into it and the curious intonation, so utterly removed from their everyday manner of speech, which they appeared to consider it necessary to adopt the moment they opened Hymns A. and M. But long before we had come to the end of the *Te Deum* this source of pleasure had begun to lose its power, and it was with a very real sense of relief that at long last I saw Canon Pelly move across in the direction of the pulpit and knew that for the next twenty minutes at least I could devote myself fully to the particular costume drama that was then running in the private theatre of my mind, undisturbed by constantly having to rise and sing or kneel and pray.

Of a sermon which was in its way to prove historic I consciously remembered, when the usual mumbled "and now to God the Father . . ." had recalled me from the broad acres where I had been grinding the faces of the Saxon peasantry in my new rôle of a Norman baron of immense strength and ferocity, not one word. Nor, had it not been for the subsequent drama at the luncheon table, would I ever have given it another thought.

On leaving church the weather which had been fine enough earlier was seen to have changed. The wind had dropped and the small white clouds of early morning had swollen and coalesced. At the best of times the dining-room at the Hall was not a cheerful apartment; the sombre red walls were not noticeably relieved by the overframed battle scenes of Wouwerman which hung there (we knew they were by Wouwerman because each contained a white horse), and the closeness of the immense beech trees to the north-facing windows cast a sullen gloom even on the sunniest day. By the time we were all seated at table the sky had become heavily overcast and with it the natural brightness which was always encouraged at Sunday luncheon.

Normally the best one could hope for by way of entertainment at this weekly ceremony was a scene provoked by my Cousin John's refusal to eat his gristle, but today I had regretfully noticed he had drawn a helping at which even one of his notorious 'daintiness' could hardly protest, and I soon abandoned myself to speculation as to whether we should receive one sweet or two at the end of the meal.

Among the grown-ups the conversation, as usual, was steered by my aunts to a discussion of this morning's sermon. It was generally agreed by those who had been privileged to hear it, that seldom had Canon Pelly been so inspired, and how lucky they were to have so eloquent and powerful a preacher in a small place like Eastwinch! Amidst the chorus of agreement which these sentiments provoked among the Grateful Hearts, Miss Redpath, who had her own opinion of Canon Pelly, maintained a menacing silence. Although it was the last day of her visit, when her patience was invariably approaching exhaustion, all might yet have been well had not one of my aunts, ignoring the danger-signals and unable to leave well alone, gone on to describe this historic sermon as "a real intellectual treat".

"Really, my dear Harriet, and pray what makes you think so?"

The use of my aunt's full name instead of the customary diminutive was a sure sign that Miss Redpath was now fully roused.

"Well," explained my aunt, rashly but with determination, "it was so wonderfully *clear*. I don't think I have ever before properly understood the parable of the labourers in the vineyard. It always seemed rather *unfair* but this morning I was made to realise its true meaning for the first time."

Miss Redpath was plainly astonished that any ex-pupil of hers could be so mentally deficient as to have gone through life failing to understand the workings of a wage system so completely in accordance with the best Trade Union practice.

"And what, dear, did the Canon choose as the text for this enlightening sermon?"

"The first shall be last and the last first."

"One hardly needs to have gone to church, dear, to know exactly what the dear Canon would have to say on that rather trite theme."

At this point my grandfather, who had been listening with a quiet enjoyment which even the snowy smoke-screen of his beard could not wholly conceal, entered the discussion. "Well, Miss Redpath, as the only person not present tell us what you think the Canon would have said."

That my grandfather realised he was playing with fire, and did so deliberately, seems fairly certain; but I doubt that even he, shrewd as he was, anticipated exactly what he got.

Miss Redpath, hands folded on her lap, leant back and after one or two preliminary flexings of the corners of her mouth, through firmly clenched teeth, began.

For the next five minutes Canon Pelly was in the room with us: every unctuous intonation, every sniff, even the faint trace of transatlantic accent that had remained to him from his missionary days in the Canadian backwoods, was faithfully reproduced. As with his elocutionary effects, so with his mental processes, all were devastatingly recorded. No cliché, no hackneyed phrase, no false argument was missed. Even I, who had been lost in private fantasies during the sermon itself, was dumbfounded at the uncanny accuracy of the performance.

When at last Miss Redpath, with a final contemptuous but still all too convincing "dearly beloved", had finished, for the first time in the recorded history of the Hall a general exodus took place without a previous request to my grandfather to say Grace. Left in the dining-room were only Miss Redpath, her host and myself. Although deeply anxious to hear my grandfather's comments, my presence was in no way an attempt to eavesdrop; but, unlike my cousins who had been plainly appalled by the whole performance and fled in panic with their elders, I had kept my head and alone of those present remembered that in the excitement the Sunday distribution of sweets had been forgotten. I was not, therefore, deliberately hiding behind the screen which half concealed the sideboard, but was principally engaged in making good this oversight, and my rôle in the last act of the drama was involuntary.

At first silence reigned. My grandfather indeed, whose whole form was heaving rhythmically beneath his beard and down whose rosy cheeks the tears were helplessly pouring, seemed incapable of speech, and contented himself with jabbing his cigar in the general direction of Miss Redpath. She for her part was smiling like the happy warrior at the end of a hard day's dragon-slaying. At long last my grandfather after many splutterings and guffaws found his voice. "You listened!"

"Of course," replied Miss Redpath smugly. "I was sitting in the porch the whole time. Not that it was really necessary. Given that particular text it was perfectly obvious to anyone of the meanest intelligence what the invincibly commonplace mind of the Canon would make of it. Still, there were one or two finer points of stupidity which even I had not foreseen."

Of this conversation one fact and one fact only stuck in my mind—Miss Redpath had listened—and I lost no time in slipping from the room and publishing the news to the world.

In the drawing-room, where I found the rest of the party assembled, a certain uneasiness reigned. Some of those present, including my mother and all **my uncles,** had obviously reacted in the same way as my grandfather, and were making little attempt to conceal their enjoyment. My aunts, on the other hand, loyally supported by the Grateful Hearts, were maintaining a strained and disapproving silence. Only on the receipt of my startling news did their brows clear.

At the time I did not understand the significance of my aunts' reaction. Now I can see that as a result of my revelation the uncertainties to which they had been prey had been resolved, and the necessary justification for action provided. So long as Miss Redpath's performance was to be regarded as a feat of creative imagination, such was their integrity and regard for intellectual honesty, that deeply as they deplored the whole scene (particularly before the children too!), they did not feel entitled to act. Now that it was made clear that her triumph had been scored as the result of eavesdropping, she stood convicted of 'playing to the gallery'. And worse: truth itself had been tampered with, for by allowing her audience to assume that she was relying entirely on brilliant speculation and concealing her presence in the porch, she had been Acting a Lie! She had, in fact, finally gone too far.

In all the long summers which I subsequently passed at the Hall, never again, by some curious chance, was it found possible so to arrange the holiday timetable as to allow Miss Redpath's visit to be fitted in to the tight schedule of the Grateful Hearts.

5. *"The last rose of Summer"*

AN AWARENESS of social distinctions is among the earliest
senses to develop in the infant mind. All children, although
in varying degrees, are snobs and if their snobbishness is
based on differences and attributes incomprehensible to the adult
mind their perception is none the less acute: which always makes
for a certain self-consciousness in the sensitive grown-up knowing
himself to be under the scrutiny of a little rompered Proust who
is weighing him up in accordance with a scale of values which,
although it may bear little relation to those of the Lord Chamber-
lain's Office or the Faubourg St. Germain, is none the less rigid
for being arbitrary. Fortunately so few grown-ups do, in fact, in
this respect appear to be sensitive.

Thus as a child I was always convinced that my maternal

grandfather Alfred was in some subtle way 'grander' than my father's father. And this in the face of a considerable amount of superficial evidence supporting the contrary view. The latter, thanks to his beard, was the more imposing in appearance, and although both were rich he was the richer; moreover not only did he possess a town house *and* a country house but had also been knighted. Nevertheless, the former's house was approached by far the longer drive and was graced by a butler, and these two distinctions, particularly the latter, I considered decisive.

Naïve as may have been the premises on which my decision was based it was nevertheless accurately indicative of a subtle difference, not so much of social position as of character, existing between the two men. Alike in the circumstances of their origins and their careers they differed completely in everything else. Both were copybook examples of the Victorian middle-class success story, but in their reactions to success no two men could have been less alike. While my Lancaster grandfather continued to work ceaselessly until almost his eightieth year, my mother's father, having made a large fortune by his early thirties, never did another hand's turn in his life. While Grandfather William gave enormous sums to charity he was always very tight-fisted when it came to tipping which made family outings to restaurants always a little embarrassing. Grandfather Alfred, on the other hand, while always adjusting his charitable benefactions strictly in accordance with what he considered the minimum obligations of a country gentleman, was noticeably lavish in the matter of casual largesse. And while both kept their offspring permanently short of cash, they did so for very different reasons: the former because he was sincerely convinced of the corrupting influence of affluence on the young, the latter because he was temperamentally opposed to anyone spending his money but himself. Moreover, while my Lancaster grandfather, despite his genealogical preoccupations, remained always the least snobbish of men scorning—indeed disapproving—all social pretensions, his opposite number had never, according to his sisters, hesitated to cut his own father when the latter was still in 'trade' on any occasion when recognition would have been an

imagined embarrassment. Alas, so desperately wicked is the heart of man and so blind to moral worth the eye of childhood, that while deeply respecting Grandfather William, my admiration for Grandfather Alfred knew no bounds.

My grandfather's great-grandfather had been a refugee who had preferred the more liberal climate of England to that prevailing in his native Marburg during the Revolutionary wars, and had settled in this country and married a lady known as 'the Rose of Shropshire' (whether or not she was so known outside the family circle I have been unable to discover). All his descendants had married in this country, and the only traces of their Teutonic origin that my mother's family still retained were exceedingly blonde colouring with very light Baltic eyes and the manuscript of a sermon allegedly preached by an ancestor, who had been Hof-Prädiger to the Elector of Hesse-Cassel, before Gustavus Adolphus on the eve of the Battle of Lützen. All that was known of their German relatives was due to a correspondence with an engaging Baron entered into by my great-grandmother which had produced a rather dull coat-of-arms with the forthright, if non-committal, motto *Ich Halte*, and a request for a loan. However, on the strength of this my great-grandfather had at one time considered adding the prefix *von* to his surname but fortunately had finally rejected the idea and thus saved his descendants considerable embarrassment in 1914.

In youth my grandfather's prospects had not been particularly rosy; his father, although in 'trade', was not very prosperously so, and all efforts to improve the family position by financial speculation had been markedly unsuccessful. A younger member of a large family he had in addition been considered delicate; but this in fact so far from being a disadvantage had proved a blessing. Thought to suffer from weak lungs it was arranged that the beardless youth should take a long sea voyage far from the fogs of South Kensington on a ship belonging to a maternal uncle who was establishing himself as a shipping magnate on the Yang-tse. Arrived in Hong-Kong he discovered that his elder brother, for whom a place had been secured in the uncle's business, was

heartily sick of the Far East and unconcealedly anxious to return. My grandfather, then barely seventeen but apparently now well set up by the sea voyage, willingly exchanged places and remained at Hong-Kong for the next fifteen years during which period he married a dashing widow, succeeded his uncle as head of the line, and made a comfortable fortune.

Of all the various subsidiary Victorian societies, firmly bound by culture and temperament to the great central organisation yet flourishing in conditions almost unimaginably different, that of the China merchants—the 'tai-pans'—must, one fancies, have been one of the most extraordinary. The picture that presents itself, founded admittedly on no detailed knowledge but rather on half-remembered gossip, on the fantastic furniture and ornaments which adorned my grandfather's house, and above all on the testimony of old photograph albums, is one that can only be compared to that of the Lusignan régime in Cyprus; a small dominant group settled on the fringe of a far older but decayed civilisation, rigidly conservative and nationalist in some things, unexpectedly assimilative in others. In the matter of clothes, for instance, no compromise appears to have been made; indeed, to judge from portraits of my grandfather at this period an almost propagandist assertiveness of Victorianism was *de rigueur*. Certainly the dundrearies would seem to be longer, the eyeglass more glistening, the neckwear heavier and more restrictive than they were even in St. James's Street. And nothing could well have made fewer concessions to local taste and conditions than Douglas Castle, the house built by the original Lepraik on the top of the Peak, a heavily machicolated granite mansion in the Scottish baronial style, in which my grandfather wed and my mother was born.

However, despite this architectural and sartorial rigidity, in other matters a far closer liaison would appear to have existed with the local culture than, say, in contemporary India. The British merchants met their Chinese colleagues on equal terms both socially and in business, and my grandfather had numerous Chinese friends, among them that Celestial Talleyrand Li-Hung-

Chang, and if cases of intermarriage were rare, less regular unions would appear to have been frequent. But the field in which the maximum co-operation would seem to have been achieved, and in which the results were most spectacular, was that of furniture design.

No generation in recorded history, with the possible exception of the Renaissance Rhinelanders, conceived beauty so exclusively in terms of ornament as did the Victorians; no race at any time has achieved so great and terrifying a mastery of intricate detail as the Chinese of the post-Ming Period; it was not therefore surprising that the resulting combination of Victorian taste and Chinese craftsmanship produced a series of objects of transcendental monstrosity of which a very large proportion appeared to have found their way into the houses of my mother's relations. The one thing which these masterpieces of tortured ingenuity had in common was a total disregard of comfort or convenience. Thus china cupboards were supplied with such a multiplicity of little shelves projecting at all levels that it was impossible to dust or remove a single object without sending six others crashing; and chairs, the lines of whose framework were, although partially blurred by an abundance of prickly carving, flowing and sinuous, would be furnished with marble seats inlaid with mother-of-pearl of the most unyielding and chilly rigidity. But of all these mixed masterpieces the most extraordinary were my grandfather's racing trophies gained at Kailoon. Here the traditional debased vase-shape common to all such objects had been retained, but in the decoration the Chinese silversmiths had been allowed the utmost licence, so that every inch of surface was covered with spirited steeplechasers conceived in the accepted Alken tradition, en-tangled with dragons, whips and horseshoes wreathed with tiger-lilies and horses' masks peering out from bamboo thickets amid clouds of butterflies, all carried out in the highest possible relief.

Our annual arrival at the maternal homestead to which the treasures of Cathay lent so individual an atmosphere was very different to our descent on Norfolk. G—, Dorset, is not among the more attractive of West Country towns: always pervaded by a smell of brewing, neither its beer nor its inhabitants enjoyed much regard in the surrounding countryside and its station, although larger, completely lacked the rustic charm of Eastwinch. Nevertheless, so keen was my anticipation of the pleasure to come, so powerful the recollected atmosphere, annually reinforced, of my grandfather's house, that the dreary yellow brick station yard had for me a quite indescribable magic. In part this was no doubt due to the presence there of the grand-paternal automobile—a dashing, crimson Talbot-Darracq that made the Lancastrian Renault appear very dowdy and dowager-like; and standing alongside it smiling, rug-laden and gleamingly gaitered, the Chauffeur Bates.

It is not uncommon for a rare degree of insight and perception to be attributed to the innocent age of childhood; instances are constantly quoted of practised deceivers who had successfully hoodwinked the shrewdest adults but whose pretences were immediately penetrated by an innocent child. If there is any truth in such assumptions I can only suppose myself to have been, in this respect at least, abnormal. For my affection for Bates, whose insolence, sycophancy and drunkenness made him detested by the whole family except my grandfather, was deep and boundless. Ruddy-complexioned, fair-moustached and, as I now realise, distressingly familiar, he continued to tyrannise over the whole household until one fatal day in 1914 when, heavily in liquor, he went too far in the presence of the son of the house returned from the Front who knocked him for six across the stable-yard. But fortunately his failings were as hidden from me as was his fate, when perched beside him on the driving seat I was borne at what seemed an unbelievable speed past the flying hedgerows up the dusty hill which led out of the town.

The gate-pillars of S—, my grandfather's residence, were also globe-topped, but this was the only thing which they had in common with those of Eastwinch Hall. Whereas the latter were, perhaps, over-prominent in view of the almost suburban drive on to which they gave, the former, half concealed by trees and shrubs, hardly suggested the long winding carriageway leading from the small Gothic lodge across the fields and finally disappearing over the hill behind a distant clump of trees. The house itself was not remarkable architecturally and exists in my memory solely as a medium-sized confusion of ivy, gables and white barge boards, but the gardens established for ever an ideal to which none subsequently encountered have ever attained. My grandfather was a skilled and enthusiastic gardener but in the style of Loudon rather than Miss Jekyll; here were none of those messy herbaceous borders and vulgar 'riots of colour' which make so many modern gardens look like the worst sort of Christmas Calendar, but terraced lawns and geometrical flower-beds symmetrically placed, their harvest of geraniums and lobelias protected by a ring of little wrought-iron hoops. Here was no crazy-paving overgrown with monstrous delphiniums stretching between sun-dial and bird-bath, but winding gravel paths arched by trellises leading to rustic summerhouses across wooden footbridges spanning contrived, fern-shaded water-falls. And the boundary was not marked by some crumbling brick wall untidy with rock-plants but by a ha-ha neatly stretched between balancing clumps of rare coniferous trees allowing a clear view across the fields to the home-farm.

The neatness and order so evident in the garden were not, curiously enough, reflected in the way of life prevailing indoors. On looking back, existence at S— has taken on rather a Tchekov flavour, but this may perhaps be due in part to art. It so happened that all my visits there in childhood seem to have been blessed with weather of exceptional heat and brightness which led, my grandfather being markedly photophobic, to the green venetian blinds being almost permanently down. This produced that filtered sub-aqueous light which, those who are old enough to remember the earliest Komisajevsky productions of Tchekov will recall, invariably flooded the country house interiors of theatrical Russia. Nevertheless, this coincidence seems to me to have reinforced rather than induced an impression which owed its origin to a certain inconsequence and lack of decision on the part of the family cast.

In strong contrast to life at Eastwinch, governed by Median

rules where no expedition or enterprise outside the normal routine was ever embarked on without the maximum planning rigidly adhered to, at S— plans were only made in order to be changed, and the whole rhythm of everyday existence was liable to be completely upset for the merest whim. Moreover while in Norfolk ill-health, anyhow in anyone under seventy, was regarded as a sign of weakness and rigorously discouraged, in Dorset no day passed without some member of the family being laid low with a migraine or a *crise de nerfs*. This was the least easily overlooked in the case of my grandfather himself for whom the stoic fortitude on which the Lancasters set so great a store made no appeal, and who saw little point in suffering if it were to be concealed and not to be shared with the largest number possible.

Thus on such days as he was attacked by one of his 'heads' the whole life of the household was completely overturned. The utmost quiet was insisted on and everyone went on tip-toe, which naturally reinforced the lugubrious effect created by the groans and bellows coming from behind his bedroom door. Within, no matter how hot the day, all the windows were tight closed, the blinds drawn and a roaring fire blazed in the grate, a condition of affairs which inevitably increased the casualty list as my grandfather could not be left alone and some member of the family had always to sit at his bedside. Even for those not so called, life was sufficiently disrupted; for, although the domestic staff was large, the constant supply of light meals on trays, most of which the invalid promptly sent back to the cook with a few acid comments and fresh instructions, the dispatch of numerous contradictory telegrams to Harley Street, all of which had to be taken by groom or chauffeur five miles to the nearest post-office, in addition to the condition of hopeless hysteria to which my grandfather sooner or later succeeded in reducing at least one of the housemaids, taxed its resources to the utmost. But while always remaining the principal sufferer, in comparison with whose agonies those of others were as nothing, my grandfather seldom remained the sole invalid for long. His second wife, although subservient to her lord in all things, was a martyr to ill health, in part genuinely so, and her children, my mother's step-sisters, had inherited from their parents the liability to take to their beds at the drop of a hat. Thus it frequently happened that I and my mother found ourselves alone for days on end, save perhaps for an uncle on vacation from Oxford or on leave from his regiment who was made of rather tougher stuff than the rest of the family.

Normally when good health was general the whole household assembled, as at Eastwinch, for the first time at family prayers, the only difference being that here absenteeism was more frequent, and less censured. The dining-room was a spacious apartment decorated in what I have always considered the appropriate style —crimson flock wallpaper, steel engravings after Gustave Doré and a massive side-board on which, together with the Chinoiserie racing-trophies, there rested at this hour a whole battery of silver dishes from which arose a gentle steam to mingle with the souls of the righteous who were being conveyed, immediately above, by a flock of angels from the moon-lit Colosseum where their earthly bodies were still being ruminatively chewed by lions. The length of the religious ceremony which preceded our own meal depended largely on whether my grandfather himself was conducting it and if so on the state of his appetite. If he had arisen brisk and early, eagerly appreciative of the whiff of fried bacon, our devotions would be carried out at breakneck speed; if, on the other hand, his night had been disturbed and he was convinced, as he frequently was, that his enfeebled health could hardly hold out much longer, the ceremony would be prolonged by the addition of a selected passage of Holy Writ read in a suitably lugubrious tone. When, as very frequently happened, the reading was taken from that passage in the Epistle to the Ephesians where the Apostle stresses the importance of submission to temporal authority the effect was immensely impressive. "Wives, submit yourselves unto your own husbands"—pause during which my grandfather's light blue eye would rest rather sorrowfully on my grandmother; " . . . children, obey your parents"—up would go the monocle and a stern glance would fall on my aunts and uncles; " . . . servants, be obedient to them that are your masters"—and it was transferred upon the ranged rows of the domestic staff. Curiously enough, I do not remember ever hearing on these occasions the verses in which the writer goes on to outline the obligations of the head of the household.

Thus spiritually purged we all sat down to an enormous and excellent breakfast which would usually pass pleasantly enough in the discussion of plans for the day which lost nothing in excitement from the knowledge that they would almost certainly not be carried out. The only interruption likely to occur was if the bacon did not attain the exact degree of crispness insisted on by my grandfather, in which case this mood of Christian resignation would vanish in a flash, and the butler would receive a brisk message for the cook, to whom, incidentally, he was married, couched in decidedly more forceful terms than those employed by Saint Paul.

For me the rest of the day passed in a series of delicious, un-organised pleasures. No one sent me on little errands; my presence was not demanded on the tennis-lawn; I was at full liberty to take what books I liked from my grandfather's library. I could spend the morning in the stable with Hodder, the groom, a splendid primeval rustic figure who had never been further than Shaftes-bury in his life, or wander unshepherded along the stream in the wood, or reconstruct the battle of Tsushima with a wooden model of the Japanese fleet, belonging to an uncle still at Wellington, in the water-tank in the kitchen garden. No one bothered me until it was time for one of the large meals which punctuated the day, and here these too were sources of keen pleasure and eager anticipa-tion; for, unlike the Lancasters, my maternal relatives were far from indifferent to what they ate and the simple country fare provided by the home-farm was reinforced by a regular supply of more exotic dainties sent down from Jacksons. All of which forces the conclusion that, on the whole, children are likely to have a far better time where the adults are reasonably self-centred.

While the enlightened self-interest, which was the guiding principle of my grandfather's life, operated happily enough in my own case, it must be confessed it showed him in rather less admirable light when dealing with other relatives. Unlike his opposite number he entertained no very exalted conception of family obligations and, apart from his own children, his affection for his relations was at its warmest when they were furthest removed, and this was particularly so in the case of his elder sister, my Great Aunt A. Left to himself, it seems likely that this remarkable old lady's visits to S— would have been even more spaced out than they were, but fortunately my mother, aided by her step-sister, was at hand to see that he did not shirk his obligations.

It must be admitted that his reluctance to entertain his sister, although undoubtedly blame-worthy, was not altogether incomprehensible. Great Aunt A was certainly, in some ways, a problem. Unmarried, her emotional life had been a series of disappointments, none the less bitter for the fact that they had been, when not wholly imaginary, largely her own fault. Her girlhood had coincided with that peculiarly sentimental period, the mid-'seventies, when clad in an art-silk bustle she had studied water-colour painting at South Kensington and lost her heart to innumerable curates. But as time went on she found a certain compensation in the extraordinary number of disagreeable encounters and impertinent suggestions to which her beauty, so she was convinced, subjected her, and she abandoned painting in favour of cultivating the more socially useful gift of a magnificent *coloratura* soprano. However, despite her blighted youth she looked forward to a dignified old age when, as she would frequently announce, she intended to put on a neat little mob-cap with lace tippets and a plain but rich watered silk dress. As at the time of her visits to S— she was invariably dressed in flowered muslins of the most youthful cut and girlish straw hats heavily over-laden with cabbage roses and was known to be close on seventy, it was not exactly clear as to when she expected the final stage of her earthly pilgrimage to begin.

My grandfather's attitude towards his sister, disgraceful as it was, was founded on a very clear-sighted appreciation of the exact nature of the caste system as it prevailed in the English country-side in the Edwardian period, and of his own position in the local hierarchy. Thanks to an engaging presence, thirty years' residence, and a stable full of hunters he was at long last established as being of 'the county' and sat on the local Bench and visited, and was visited by, all the neighbouring landowners. Nevertheless, he fully realised that there were still subtle distinctions within the closed circle into which he had been at such pains to enter, and whereas the local baronet, whose family had been resident in the neighbourhood for generations, could easily afford the presence beneath his roof of any number of the most wildly eccentric female relations, unfavourable comment was only too likely to be aroused by any too great prominence attaching to the mildly ridiculous elder sister of a retired China merchant. Eccentricity, to be socially acceptable, had still to have at least four or five generations of inbreeding behind it.

Thus, during the period of Great Aunt A's visit there was always a marked reduction in the number of little luncheon-parties for the local gentry and my grandfather's health would seldom permit his attendance at church on Sunday. In the latter instance his lack of moral fibre was, perhaps, forgivable, for even those with nerves of iron might well be shaken on finding themselves in the close proximity of Great Aunt A at Divine Service. For not only did that indomitable old lady always on these occasions take particular pains with her dress which led to the most fantastic superfluity of large pale blue bows, dangling ear-rings and enormous brooches strategically placed, but invariably made the most of the opportunity afforded for the fullest exercise of her remarkable voice. All was moderately well so long as she sang in unison; gradually almost complete silence would fall on the neighbouring pews as they realised the uselessness of competition, and one or two of the more impressionable choir-boys would collapse in hysterics, though a semblance of harmony was maintained; but once she started to sing seconds, as sooner or later she invariably did, all hope was lost and the organist could do nothing but immediately switch to $f\!f$ and put on what speed he could, hoping for the best. Then it was that the more stalwart members of the family thought enviously of its head, comfortably tucked up in bed reading Meredith, and wondered whether or not their own displays of unflinching loyalty had really been worth it.

In addition to her vocal enthusiasm and bizarre taste in dress, Great Aunt A brought with her another cause of disruption. Like many maiden ladies living alone her affection for her domestic pets had long since passed way beyond the limits of normality, and all the passion which the curates had so unthinkingly rejected was now directed on her canary and her Pekinese. The former, whose vocal range was even more piercingly extended than Great Aunt A's own, was fortunately left behind, together with endless instructions and ample supplies of groundsel, with the landlady (to whom numerous admonitory post-cards on the subject of fresh water and cage-cleaning would regularly be dispatched) but the latter invariably accompanied his mistress on all her travels. Even by Pekinese standards, which in my experience are exalted, Mr. Wu rated as a menace of the highest order. Ostentatiously conscious of his aristocratic breeding, like so many of the bluest blood, he made no effort to conceal his arrogance and selfishness, and regarded it as completely absolving him from all effort to conform to the usages of decent canine society. House training was only for the middle-classes and he constantly dirtied carpets and chintz with all the insouciance of Louis XIV relieving himself in the open fireplace at Versailles. In addition he gloried in the possession of a delicate digestion and not only insisted on the most tender meals but threw up his dinner with an uninhibited frequency when and where he chose. His temper was as uncontrolled as his personal habits and despite the aristocratic flatness of his features he was perfectly capable of producing a nasty flesh wound at ankle level. In no house, therefore, was Mr. Wu a welcome guest, but at my grandfather's his presence always proved more than usually disruptive, as here, for probably the only times in his life, he encountered stiff opposition.

S—, like so many houses wherein all summer-long there reigns a thwarted restlessness due to the fact that for the majority of the inhabitants life only begins with the hunting season, was heavily over-dogged, as if a constant yapping and baying, faint echoes of the glorious music of the winter-months, was absolutely necessary to maintain vitality during a period insufficiently enlivened by tennis parties: and despite the constant protests of my grandfather, who was no friend to the lower orders of creation and for whom the hunting field had a purely social justification, vast hordes of his offsprings' pets constantly roamed the whole place. In the case of my Uncle Jack's spaniels, Budge and Toddy, as kindly and affectionate as their master, the rule barring entry to the house itself was fairly strictly observed; with the fox-terrier Jacky who had developed a mania for snapping off the heads of chickens (and with great speed and skill, for I well remember the surrealist

spectacle of several headless birds all running round the farm-yard at once) a certain feeling of relief was induced by his presence indoors; but over my youngest aunt's kennel no control had ever been effectively achieved. This last usually consisted of at least half a dozen Sealyhams, of unbounded energy and considerable ferocity, and a couple of Irish wolf-hounds, friendly and amiable enough, but one friendly wag of whose tails was capable of obliterating a whole regiment of netsukés and any quantity of Satsuma ware. Thus life was constantly being enlivened by a series of appalling scenes between parents and children and brothers and sisters arising from vain attempts to establish the exact responsibility for the latest canine misdemeanour. Sometimes, as when half-way through a smart little luncheon party at which my grandfather was entertaining an important local magnate all the cream for the strawberries was discovered to have been devoured by Jacky, these reached epic proportions and went rumbling on for years. On other occasions, such as when the new curate paying his first call had been brought down on the drawing-room carpet by the whole pack of Sealyhams in full cry and rescued only just in the nick of time, the incident passed off in peals of happy laughter and soon became a favourite subject for joyous reminiscence. With the arrival of Mr. Wu the incidence of such disasters not only immensely increased but, owing to Great Aunt A's almost insane affection for her repellent hound, left a trail of much intensified bitterness behind them. And it was to a disaster thus brought about that I owed my earliest acquaintance with one of the fundamental, and least agreeable, facts of life.

The garden at S— had been laid out on a slight incline, the ground falling away from the highest point outside the drawing-room windows to the ha-ha which marked the boundary of the level fields, and in order to accommodate both a croquet-lawn and a tennis court two fairly steep cuttings had been made so that the terrace was separated from the tennis and the tennis from the croquet by neatly turfed embankments of considerable height and steepness. One fine morning I was pleasantly engaged in rolling down the upper and steeper of these two ramps—an occupation to which I had devoted much practice and in which, while giving a gratifying illusion of distress to uninformed witnesses, I was able to indulge with no hurt or inconvenience to myself—in the indulgent charge of Great Aunt A who was reading *Home Chat* in a deck-chair on the terrace. Alongside her and slobbering over a disgusting rubber ball was Mr. Wu, who had only been allowed to expose himself to the perils of the outer world on the strict understanding that all the various gates and doors which gave access from this part of the garden to the stable-yard, to which the rest of the canine population had been banished, were securely locked.

Quite suddenly the desultory barking which formed an almost continuous ground-bass to the confused melody of our daily life became much louder and more purposeful and almost before I or

Great Aunt A had fully registered this fact, the whole pack of Sealyhams came skidding round the geraniums in full cry. The reason for their sudden appearance was not for a second in doubt to any of us, least of all Mr. Wu, whose fully justified fears of a *jacquerie* he at last saw terrifyingly realised. With one bound he was

on his mistress' lap only to be immediately snatched up by my terrified aunt and clasped tight to her shoulder as far out of the aggressors' range as possible. They, however, quite obviously meant business; their views of the mandarin-class coincided exactly with those of Sun-Yat-Sen and they were clearly in no doubt at all as to who was the cause of their enforced seclusion of the last few days. Realising, after a few abortive leaps, that their predestined victim was out of reach, they changed their tactics and concentrated on getting his protectress down. I, meanwhile, seeing that the Sealyhams, of whom I entertained a healthy and not unjustified dread, were at the moment quite single-minded, gave myself up to a fascinated contemplation of Great Aunt A in the lead-rôle of 'Fireman save my child', from which her frenzied shrieks of "Osbert, don't just sit there! *Do* Something!" quite failed to rouse me. The end was inevitable and terrifying; my great aunt, her tartan skirt already loosened from its moorings, still clutching her darling whose aristocratic calm had for once, I was happy to observe, quite deserted him, backed steadily towards the edge of the terrace. One moment she was aloft and upright, assailed, frightened but still dominant—the next she was falling helpless through the air to land backwards on the croquet-lawn only a split second before the whole pack had galloped down the incline on top of her. At the exact moment that she lost her balance a shocking truth was suddenly made apparent to me; that grown-ups, whom I had always regarded as exempt from falling down and hurting themselves, were as liable to physical mishaps as children, and that being grown-up did not automatically give one complete and certain control over all events whatsoever. Then the fear so clearly discernible in the eyes of poor Aunt A aroused an echo in my own heart, chilly and far-reaching.

* * * * *

All too soon our visit would come to an end. One day a complicated timetable would be worked out in which my grandfather's visit to the dentist in Bath could conveniently be combined with our catching the fast train to London, readjusted to allow of my aunt's taking one of the Sealyhams to the vet in Wincanton, a picnic *en route* substituted for luncheon at the Grand Pump Room Hotel, and finally abandoned entirely amidst a storm of argument and counter-suggestions. In due course the car would come round to take us to G— station as usual and I would be led up to take leave of my grandfather, trying hard not to look expectant but always nevertheless relieved on hearing the faint crackle of a fiver as my hand was warmly shaken, provoking profuse thanks from me and distressed cries of "Really, Father, you shouldn't! It's far too much!" from my mother, and, I am deeply ashamed to say, in the depths of my heart scornful reflections on my grandfather Lancaster who on such occasions (which I did not pause to consider were in his case far more numerous) seldom rose to more than half a sovereign.

In the homeward train I was always a prey to the deepest gloom from which neither the latest *Rainbow* nor the arrival of the luncheon basket with the inevitable leg of L.S.W.R. chicken, strangely blue in colour, could rouse me. No more long afternoons reading Kenneth Grahame in the hammock, no more ponies, no more young and indulgent aunts and uncles, no more making myself sick on lemonade in the butler's pantry—even the prospect of once more seeing Kate could not compensate for all I was losing. At last I could bear it no longer and would angrily demand in a voice not far from tears why, when I was so happy, did we have to come away? Gentle but firm the answer was always the same, "Osbert dear, you are old enough now to realise that we are not put into this world just to be happy."